MONTRĒAL

L'ouvrage illustré sur les Jeux Olympiques de 1976

LA PUBLICATION OFFICIELLE DE L'ASSOCIATION OLYMPIQUE CANADIENNE

The Pictorial Record of the 1976 Olympic Games

THE OFFICIAL PUBLICATION OF THE CANADIAN OLYMPIC ASSOCIATION

Les jeux
Olympiques d'été
The Summer
Olympic Games
Die Olympishen
Sommerspiele
I Giochi Estivi

MONT

proSport CANADA PUBLICATIONS LTD/LTÉE

RĒAL 76

Photographie/Photography Toby Rankin +
Robert Burch, Ted Grant, Joe di Maggio, David Paterson,
Fred Stevenson, Michael Taylor & Robert Warren

Conception Graphique/Concept and Design Frank Newfeld

DIRECTEUR DU PROJET
PROJECT DIRECTOR
Edgar Spallek

DIRECTEUR ARTISTIQUE
CREATIVE DIRECTOR
Frank Newfeld

COORDINATEUR
DE LA PRODUCTION
PRODUCTION COORDINATOR
Afzal R. Rahman

MARKETING
Michael R. Aldercotte

ADJOINTS:
ASSISTANTS:
Karin Adolf
Madeleine Bourgault
Wendy Brown
Christine Cerro
Ingrid Grimpe
Cecil La Bel
Ursula Lampart
Diane Mew

© proSport Canada
Publications Ltd/Lteé
1976

ISBN 0-920172-04-0

A **proSport** PUBLICATION
2125 rue Crescent Street
Montréal   Canada

IMPRIMÉ ET RELIÉ AU CANADA PAR
PRINTED AND BOUND IN CANADA BY
The Hunter Rose Company

Table des matières
Contents

CITIUS-ALTIUS-FORTIUS

PLUS VITE, PLUS HAUT, PLUS FORT	SWIFTER, HIGHER, STRONGER	SCHNELLER, HÖHER, STÄRKER	PIU AGILE, PIU GRANDE, PIU FORTE
La devise olympique conçue par **Le Père Didon** Directeur Collège Arcueil France, 1895	The Olympic Motto conceived by **Father Didon** Headmaster Arcueil College France, 1895	Das Olympische Motto geprägt von **Pater Didon** Rektor des Kollegiums Arcueil Frankreich, 1895	Il motto delle Olimpiade ideato da **Padre Didon** Preside del Collegio Arcueil Francia, 1895

REMERCIEMENTS

ACKNOWLEDGEMENTS

Nous dédions ce livre en hommage à tous nos athlètes qui ont participé aux Jeux olympiques de Montréal. Grace à la publication de ce livre, nos athlètes ont bénéficié d'un octroi de $100,000. Nos remerciements s'adressent aux nombreuses personnes, organisations et sociétes lesquelles ont participées aux succès de ce livre en y souscrivant et en accordant leur appui moral.

This book is dedicated with pride to all our amateur athletes who participated in these Olympic Games. A grant of $100,000. for the benefit of the athletes has been made possible by the publication of this book. We wish to thank the many individuals, organizations and companies who helped to make this book a success, both by subscribing to it and by giving us their moral support.

GÉRANTE DES VENTES-QUÉBEC
SALES MANAGER-QUÉBEC
Madeleine Bourgault

GÉRANT DES VENTES-ONTARIO
SALES MANAGER-ONTARIO
Murray Tildesley

REPRÉSENTANTS
REPRESENTATIVES
Judy Bradley
Joy Brown
Betty-Lou Dubord
Anne Fleming
Peggy Fleming
Louise Germain
Kima Grieve
Ingrid Grimpe
Adele Hamilton
Cheryl Kardish
Chantal Lesage
Anne MacRory
Kathy Peacock
Leesa Smith
Lizette Surprenant
Hilda Yaffe

REPRÉSENTANTS
REPRESENTATIVES
John Boothroyd
Toni Cameron
Ronald Crawford
Wendy Dobson
Bill Dowbiggin
Sandi Fleming
Marguerite McKinnon
Wendy Main
Laurie Marshall
Anna Nordine
Lynn Parker
Virginia Rowlands
William Rundle
Anna Spencer
Brenda Tiller
Jackie Woolsey

Montréal Accueille

ontréal constitue maintenant un relais inoubliable sur la voie des Jeux olympiques.» Réflexion fort juste d'un commentateur français de retour dans son pays après les Jeux de la XXIe Olympiade dans la deuxième ville française du monde. Grâce à une ténacité exceptionnelle, à une volonté de fer et à un travail de géant, Montréal a pu, du 17 juillet au 1er août, accueillir plus de 3 millions et demi de spectateurs aux divers sites de compétitions. «C'est un peu de votre patrie que nous avons l'impression d'avoir emporté à la semelle de nos souliers» poursuivait ce journaliste de France soulignant bien par là l'accueil chaleureux que lui fit Montréal.

Lorsque l'ancien président du CIO, le regretté Avery Brundage, annonça le 12 mai 1970 que Montréal serait l'hôte des Jeux olympiques en 1976, la métropole du Canada reçut la nouvelle dans une euphorie collective. Cependant, cette même euphorie devait par la suite s'effriter et faire place à un pessimisme et un négativisme entérinés par un grand nombre de Canadiens. Mais pour le maire de Montréal Jean Drapeau le défi était de taille; à la grandeur même de sa pensée, de sa volonté. Dès le tout début, des résistances se firent sentir dans plusieurs milieux, surtout lorsque fut connu le choix d'un architecte français, Roger Taillibert, dont le concept devait s'avérer par la suite un véritable chef-d'oeuvre architectural qui attirera encore longtemps à Montréal des visiteurs venant de partout pour admirer cette merveilleuse cité sportive de l'avenir.

La mise en chantier devait se faire sans trop de heurts, mais dans les mois qui suivirent, les arrêts de travail, les grèves et le sabotage ont grandement mis en cause l'échéance des constructions; à tel point qu'un peu partout on répétait sans cesse que Montréal ne serait jamais prête à temps pour présenter les Jeux. D'ailleurs, à la suite d'une publicité des plus négatives répandue en Europe surtout, à Munich on se préparait déjà à imiter Innsbruck qui avait pris la relève lorsque Denver s'était désisté pour les Jeux d'hiver. Face à l'échéancier qui n'offrait aucune alternative, divers groupes ont utilisé ce tremplin pour le marchandage, ce qui a eu pour effet de faire grimper les coûts de construction de façon astronomique.

LE STADE

Entreprise architecturale fort audacieuse, le stade olympique est entièrement nouveau, depuis sa conception jusqu'à sa réalisation ultime. Il pourra être utilisé en toute saison puisqu'on procède déjà à l'achèvement du mât géant qui soutiendra le toit amovible.

Le stade, pendant les Jeux, a pu accueillir plus de 70,000 personnes et sa capacité sera maintenant réduite à 56,000 sièges alors qu'il accueillera le football professionnel canadien et le baseball majeur avec les Expos de Montréal. C'est dans ce stade qu'ont eu lieu les cérémonies d'ouverture et de clôture, toutes les épreuves d'athlétisme ainsi que les demi-finales et la finale du football, sans oublier le Grand Prix équestre de sauts d'obstacles par équipes.

Les 18 épreuves d'athlétisme ont attiré 934,624 spectateurs, contre 503,863 pour le football, dont 342,619 au stade même. Sous la base du grand mât se trouve la piscine olympique qui comprend un bassin de natation de 50 m x 25 m x 2 m, à 10 couloirs; un bassin de plongeon avec plates-formes à 10 m, 7 m et 5 m et tremplins de 3 m et 1 m; un bassin d'entraînement et un bassin de plongée sous-marine.

L'édifice a pu accueillir 9,200 spectateurs pendant les Jeux mais ce total sera maintenant réduit à 2,500 places permanentes.

Un gymnase, des saunas, des salles de repos et de massage, un centre médical, des installations de contrôle électronique, un centre de réception et une cafétéria complètent l'ensemble.

Les 19 épreuves qui s'y sont déroulées ont attiré 159,506 spectateurs.

LE VÉLODROME

Tout juste à côté et relié directement à la piscine et au grand stade, se trouve le fantastique vélodrome, édifice qui ressemble étrangement de l'extérieur à une crevette géante, surtout à cause de la forme de son toit à panneaux de verre acrylique.

Sa piste de bois est de 285.714 mètres. Les compétitions de judo se sont déroulées au centre de cette piste. Cette même surface sera maintenant recouverte par une patinoire de glace artificielle.

Le vélodrome entièrement climatisé peut accueillir entre 7,000 et 10,000 spectateurs. Pour les 6 compétitions de cyclisme, 35,318 personnes se sont massées dans les estrades.

Les 12 épreuves de judo ont attiré 63,255 amateurs de ces combats.

LE BASSIN D'AVIRON

Le bassin d'aviron, virtuellement taillé à même le site de l'Exposition universelle de 1967 et la Voie maritime, a reçu pour les 13 compétitions, 77,927 personnes.

LES COMPÉTITIONS

L'une des belles surprises fut certes le basketball, alors qu'au Canada il n'existe aucun circuit majeur ou professionnel dans cette discipline. Les spectateurs au nombre de 83,822 ont pris place dans les gradins du tout nouveau centre Etienne-Desmarteau pour assister aux 21 rencontres, tandis que les demi-finales et les finales ont à leur tour attiré 97,005 mordus au Forum de Montréal. Le Centre Etienne-Desmarteau fut ainsi nommé en l'honneur du premier athlète canadien à mériter une médaille d'or olympique.

Dans le domaine de la boxe, à l'aréna Maurice-Richard dédiée au plus célèbre joueur de hockey de tous les temps, 121,858 amateurs ont assisté aux 24 compétitions, alors que les finales au Forum en ont attiré 17,497, ce qui fait un bon total de 139,355 spectateurs.

Que dire de l'enthousiasme des 213,702 spectateurs témoins des prodiges de Nadia Comaneci et autres gymnastes au Forum, de l'emballement des 60,972 personnes présentes lors des compétitions de handball au Palais des Sports à Sherbrooke, à l'Université Laval à Québec, au centre Claude-Robillard et au Forum à Montréal?

Que dire aussi du basketball qui a été une révélation pour beaucoup de Montréalais?

Il en a été de même pour les rencontres de hockey sur gazon alors que 126,663 personnes se rendaient au stade Molson de l'Université McGill.

Quand à l'haltérophilie, à l'aréna Saint-Michel, 34,551 fervents de ce sport ont assisté aux 17 épreuves dans un édifice malheureusement beaucoup trop petit.

L'assistance totale aux 8 compétitions de water polo a été de 90,500 personnes.

A Bromont, dans les Cantons de l'Est, à une centaine de kilomètres de la métropole, on a compté 15,000 personnes pour la phase équestre du pentathlon moderne et 131,043 autres spectateurs pour les compétitions.

Si les épreuves de tir n'ont attiré que 6,629 personnes au site de l'Acadie, sur la rive sud du fleuve Saint-Laurent, à une trentaine de kilomètres seulement du site olympique, 12,796 spectateurs pour le tir à l'arc se sont rendus à Joliette, à 50 kilomètres de Montréal. Cet endroit est considéré comme l'un des plus beaux clubs de tir à l'arc au monde.

Ajoutons à cette nomenclature, 211,011 personnes intéressées par le volleyball au centre Paul-Sauvé et au Forum et 24,758 autres spectateurs pour l'escrime à l'Université de Montréal; si l'on pense également aux plus de 70,000 personnes assistant aux cérémonies d'ouverture et aux 136,116 autres présentes lors de la journée finale et de la cérémonie de clôture, on atteint facilement un grand total dépassant les 3,316,420 privilégiés qui ont pu assister aux Jeux alors que souvent les billets de dernière minute se vendaient clandestinement à prix d'or aux entrées du stade ou ailleurs. Certains ont même versé jusqu'à $200 canadiens pour un seul billet pour la journée d'ouverture et un montant à peu près identique pour la cérémonie de clôture.

CÉRÉMONIES D'OUVERTURE – GESTE HISTORIQUE

Les représentants de la Grèce, pays d'origine des Jeux, ouvrant la marche, des athlètes de tous les pays participants ont défilé au son du concept musical tiré de l'oeuvre du regretté André Mathieu, sur des arrangements de Victor Vogel et Art Philipps.

Son Excellence Monsieur Roger Rousseau, président du COJO et Commissaire général des Jeux, a présenté Lord Killanin, président du CIO, et invité sa Majesté la Reine Elisabeth d'Angleterre, accompagnée du Duc d'Edimbourg, à ouvrir officiellement les Jeux de la XXIe Olympiade tenus pour la première fois en terre canadienne et pour la deuxième fois en Amérique; les Jeux de 1932 ayant eu lieu à Los Angeles.

Des danseurs munichois et montréalais se sont unis pour présenter une fresque composée de thèmes folkloriques de leurs pays respectifs.

Le drapeau olympique passa ensuite des mains du maire de Munich à celle de Lord Killanin puis à celle du maire Jean Drapeau. Au moment de transmettre à son tour ce drapeau à l'un des danseurs, le maire de Montréal a eu un moment d'hésitation et l'a plutôt penché en direction de la foule. Ce simple geste a provoqué une émotion telle dans l'assistance que celle-ci fit spontanément une ovation monstre à cet homme trop souvent critiqué et qui venait pourtant de doter Montréal, le Québec et, le Canada d'installations sportives fantastiques et qui demeurent un chef-d'oeuvre d'architecture moderne.

CÉRÉMONIES DE CLÔTURE

La cérémonie de clôture a donné lieu à un défilé difficile à décrire tellement il était riche en couleurs.

Des milliers d'Indiens aux costumes flamboyants évoquaient bien les origines amérindiennes du Canada. Au cours d'un ballet folklorique, toujours aux vibrants accents de la musique d'André Mathieu, les danseurs indiens ont en un tour de main érigé des tentes aux couleurs des continents, au beau milieu de cinq cercles formés par des centaines de danseuses vêtues de costumes aux couleurs olympiques.

Au moment ou Lord Killanin, chargé de proclamer la clôture officielle des Jeux, fit mention de remerciements dus au COJO, à la Ville de Montréal, au maire Drapeau, ses paroles ont déclenché une frénésie collective telle que, cette fois encore, la foule fit à ce dernier une ovation délirante. Cet hommage bien mérité venait enfin rendre justice à sa ténacité, à sa détermination.

Vers la fin de la cérémonie, sitôt après la descente des drapeaux, la foule, dans un élan d'enthousiasme, envahit la piste du stade, se mêlant aux participants. Tout le monde a dansé, chanté, s'est embrassé dans une explosion d'amitié et de fraternité sans précédent. Cette fin de cérémonie n'avait certes pas été prévue au programme de la journée mais une manifestation aussi sincère et spontanée a été le témoignage le plus vivant, le plus vibrant, de la réussite de cette entreprise titanesque et demeurera un souvenir impérissable des Jeux de la XXIᵉ Olympiade à Montréal pour tous ceux qui l'ont vécu.

Au centre équestre de Bromont, à celui du tir à l'arc de Joliette et au centre de voile de Kingston, en Ontario, des cérémonies de clôture ont eu lieu, plus modestes mais tout aussi pittoresques.

AU REVOIR!

Il est certain que les Montréalais ont mis tout leur coeur à préparer un accueil fraternel à tous les athlètes et que les Jeux, à ce point de vue, ont atteint leur but.

Les étrangers qui ont quitté Montréal, comme les Montréalais qui les ont regardé partir, éprouvaient tous, sans doute, le même sentiment de nostalgie, tempéré par l'espoir des retrouvailles, pour la XXIIᵉ Olympiade à Moscow.

Mission Accomplie

Les Jeux olympiques de Montréal ont été merveilleusement réussis.» C'est ainsi qu'au lendemain de la cérémonie de clôture des Jeux s'est exprimé dans un élan d'enthousiasme Lord Michael Killanin, président du Comité international olympique, lui qui pendant quatre ans appréhendait le pire. Jeux bien réussis, organisés avec un synchronisme exceptionnel à un rythme soutenu, sans conteste ... mais à quel prix? Combien de sacrifices avant, pendant et surtout après les Jeux, les Montréalais et les Québécois ont dû accepter et devront encore consentir pour que la métropole du Canada maintienne aux yeux de tous, sa vocation internationale, son caractère définitif de carrefour mondial en Amérique du Nord?

Lorsque le maire Jean Drapeau apprenait à Amsterdam, le 12 mai 1970, que Montréal était choisie pour présenter les Jeux olympiques d'été de 1976, la métropole canadienne acceptait ce défi incroyable. Défi relevé en dépit de multiples difficultés face à la construction, aux grèves, aux arrêts de travail et également au négativisme, au scepticisme de trop de gens. Réussite et tour de force même devant un virtuel abandon du reste du pays pour qui les Jeux signifiaient une exclusivité montréalaise qu'on n'avait pas à endosser ou à aider tout en se gardant bien le privilège de chercher à en récolter les fruits.

Montréal, métropole du Canada, centre nerveux du Québec et deuxième plus grande ville française au monde, aura permis à l'univers de vivre des heures inoubliables grâce à l'Organisation de radio-télévision des olympiques (ORTO), diffuseur-hôte des Jeux de la XXIᵉ Olympiade, à Montréal en 1976, qui a effectué le reportage des 21 sports au programme et dans les 27 lieux des compétitions des Jeux. L'ORTO a assuré aux diffuseurs canadiens et étrangers dûment accrédités par le Comité organisateur des Jeux olympiques (COJO) les signaux internationaux de son et d'image devant leur permettre de transmettre les Jeux au Canada et de par le monde. Images sensationnelles d'un événement frôlant la perfection.

LE VILLAGE DES ATHLÈTES

Déjà conscients de cette visite «mondiale» pour l'avoir accueillie lors de l'Exposition universelle de 1967, les deux millions de Montréalais ont reçu les athlètes et les délégués avec chaleur et spontanéité.

Dans ce village dont l'architecture s'est inspirée des pyramides d'Egypte, 113 pays se sont regroupés dans la joie et l'allégresse. Ce noyau composé de 9,514 personnes dont

5,138 athlètes masculins et 1,376 athlètes féminines, comprenait également 2,980 accompagnateurs et délégués. Sans compter cette Journée internationale de presse pendant laquelle tout journaliste accrédité fut admis librement dans l'enceinte du village, on a accueilli en tout 10,053 journalistes et près de 32,000 visiteurs.

A l'heure du départ, c'est sans doute M. Claude Collard, président du Comité olympique de France, qui a le mieux exprimé les sentiments de la masse venue des quatre coins du monde s'abriter sous la double pyramide, lorsqu'il a déclaré: «Les mesures de protection des athlètes mises en place ont donné raison aux autorités canadiennes. Nous désirons adresser au COJO, à la ville de Montréal, au maire Jean Drapeau en particulier, au Québec, au Canada, de très vives félicitations et de chaleureux remerciements pour leur magistrale organisation et leur généreux accueil.» M. Collard a poursuivi en disant que «les mesures de protection ont assuré le parfait déroulement des Jeux et évité tout incident qui aurait pu être dramatique pour l'avenir des Jeux olympiques. Ces mesures ont été appliquées avec tant de courtoisie et de gentillesse qu'athlètes et dirigeants n'y ont plus prêté attention très vite. Ainsi, les athlètes de tous les pays ont pu en toute sérénité s'exprimer totalement et encore une fois étonner le monde par des performances admirables.»

Laissons au maire du Village, M. Yvan Dubois, le soin de résumer en une phrase sa pensée sur la situation: «C'est la jeunesse québécoise qui a fait les Jeux, qui a créé l'ambiance, maintenu l'organisation efficace, et cette jeunesse, la nôtre, a merveilleusement bien relevé le grand défi.»

L'ALLER-RETOUR AFRICAIN

Si les Jeux de 1972 à Munich avaient attiré 122 pays, 91 se sont disputé les honneurs des compétitions en sol québécois. Des 29 pays à déclarer forfait, 23 se trouvaient déjà installés dans l'enceinte du Village. Les pays africains, à l'exception de cinq, ont quitté la métropole sans avoir participé au défilé d'ouverture ni aux compétitions. Les cinq pays demeurés jusqu'à la fin sont le Sénégal, la Côte d'Ivoire, la Gambie, la République Centrafricaine et le Malawi. Tous les autres se sont retirés dans un geste de solidarité pour protester contre la présence de l'équipe de la Nouvelle-Zélande à Montréal. Les Africains réclamaient le renvoi des membres de l'équipe de ce pays en raison de la présence d'un club de ce même pays en Afrique du Sud, le pays de l'apartheid. D'ailleurs, tous ces retraits, à l'exception de San Salvador étaient le résultat de la politique. Ainsi, à cause de ces multiples départs, 684 athlètes et accompagnateurs n'ont jamais participé aux Jeux.

Les véritables fervents du grand sport amateur ont été privés de quelques duels d'envergure mondiale. Ainsi, John Akii-Bua, de l'Ouganda, champion de Munich dans le 400 mètres haies, et le Tunisien Mohammed Gam-moudi, médaille d'or de Mexico dans les 5,000 mètres, n'ont jamais foulé la piste du grand stade. Il en a été de même pour Filbert Bayi, de la Tanzanie, détenteur du record mondial du 1500 mètres. Ce retrait a permis à son grand rival de toujours, le Néo-Zélandais John Walker, de venir cueillir la médaille d'or au podium sans avoir eu à vaincre Bayi.

Pour citer un journaliste du Congo, demeuré sur place jusqu'à la fin des compétitions: «Pour nos athlètes, ce furent les Jeux de l'aller-retour.» Malgré l'absence de ces Noirs, en réalité le départ de tout un continent, les Jeux de Montréal auront connu un succès retentissant tant par leur organisation, les exploits en piste et les nombreux records en natation que par l'engouement du grand public pour toutes les disciplines sans exception.

L'INCIDENT TAIWAN

L'incident Taiwan aura été le premier à marquer les Jeux par la politique. A quelques semaines de l'ouverture, le gouvernement canadien a de nouveau fait connaître sa décision de ne pas accepter l'équipe de Taiwan à titre de représentant officiel de la Chine, reconnaissant officiellement depuis longtemps la Chine rouge de Mao comme unique mandataire investi de ce titre.

Dans un effort ultime pour permettre la représentation taiwanaise, le gouvernement fédéral a accepté l'hymne national et le drapeau emblématique sans toutefois céder à l'appellation «République de Chine», concédant cependant les lettres ROC, ce que les délégués de Taiwan ont refusé. Ainsi, après s'être rendus jusqu'à Boston, les athlètes ont dû retourner chez eux sans même entrer au Canada. Aux yeux des observateurs, et même du Comité international olympique, la concession gouvernementale semblait adéquate mais à Taïpé, on s'est refusé à ce compromis, ce qui a fait couler énormément d'encre pour bien peu.

LE CAS BERLIOUX

Il y eut aussi ces remarques acerbes de la part de Mme Monique Berlioux, secrétaire générale du CIO, à l'endroit des Montréalais et des Québécois, à l'effet que les Jeux manquaient de chaleur humaine, que la ville n'était pas pavoisée adéquatement, que les Canadiens n'avaient pas su s'imprégner de l'esprit olympique et qu'ils ne connaissaient pas les subtilités des sports olympiques. Cette déclaration eut l'effet d'une véritable bombe et souleva l'ire de tous et chacun, encore plus chez les nombreux personnages impliqués à tous les paliers de l'organisation. Leurs vives protestations ne se sont pas fait attendre afin d'affirmer le contraire.

UNE PREMIÈRE

Dans l'après-midi du samedi 17 juillet, masse grouillante, plus de 70,000 personnes s'entassaient pour assister à la cérémonie d'ouverture des Jeux de la XXIe Olympiade. Pas un seul siège de libre et même en plusieurs endroits, on parvenait à partager à deux le petit espace réglementaire. Au son de la musique de cet enfant prodige du Québec, André Mathieu, le défilé des délégations a connu un succès extraordinaire. Puis Montréal a innové. Pour la première fois dans l'histoire olympique, ce sont deux jeunes coureurs, au lieu d'un seul, qui ont pénétré dans l'enceinte du grand stade, porteurs de la flamme sacrée. Le Comité organisateur des Jeux a voulu ainsi souligner la présence des deux cultures en terre canadienne. Stéphane Préfontaine, de Montréal, et la jolie Sandra Henderson, de Toronto, deux jeunes athlètes qui avaient participé aux épreuves de qualification en vue des Jeux, ont donc été choisis pour cet insigne honneur. C'est ainsi que fut reléguée aux oubliettes, la tradition qui voulait jusqu'à ce jour qu'un ancien champion olympique entre seul au stade avec le flambeau.

Cette flamme venue d'Olympie via Athènes et Ottawa, devait ainsi brûler dans la vasque du grand stade pendant tous les Jeux sans qu'un seul incident fâcheux ne vienne gâter le spectacle. Lorsque le drapeau brodé en Belgique, emblème des Jeux, est passé des mains du maire de Munich, M. Georg Kronawitter, à celles du maire de Montréal, M. Jean Drapeau, le premier magistrat de la métropole a reçu une première ovation monstre alors que la foule de plus de 70,000 personnes s'est levée spontanément.

Jean Drapeau devenait le premier maire de l'histoire moderne à pouvoir assister aux Jeux alors qu'il occupait toujours le poste de premier citoyen de la ville hôtesse. Les ovations dont il devait être l'objet à la cérémonie de clôture confirmaient la reconnaissance d'un peuple envers cet homme aux remarquables talents de bâtisseur. Cet homme même qui a dû subir pendant des années des critiques fusant de toutes parts, sans oublier les conflits ouvriers et politiques. Des Jeux de Montréal, Jean Drapeau est sorti plus grand encore.

Politique, construction, organisation, protocole, cérémonies, tout cédait enfin place aux athlètes. Tant dans l'enceinte du grand stade qu'à tous les autres sites des compétitions; les exploits se multipliaient, les records tombaient et les performances côtoyaient l'incroyable, la perfection. C'était un peu comme si on avait voulu profiter de l'occasion pour atteindre l'ultime dans l'effort ou le résultat parfait.

REINE DES JEUX

C'est une fillette touchée par la baguette magique des fées qui aura donné le ton aux performances extraordinaires.

Venue d'un petit village de Roumanie, âgée à peine de 15 ans, Nadia Comaneci aura laissé aux yeux du monde entier la marque indélibile, inoubliable, d'un talent virtuellement impossible à croire et comprendre chez une enfant beaucoup plus à l'âge de jouer avec une poupée qu'à celui d'émerveiller l'univers par des prouesses en gymnastique.

Quittant l'enceinte du Forum pour la dernière fois, cette Roumaine, qui a peut-être quelque peu perdu le sourire devant l'effort surhumain exigé d'elle, rapportait sans doute ce que jusqu'alors on avait crû impossible. Jamais dans le passé, un jury olympique n'avait osé accorder une marque parfaite de 10 dans l'une ou l'autre discipline... et pourtant Nadia Comaneci a quitté le sol canadien avec sept marques parfaites, sans oublier 3 médailles d'or, une d'argent et une autre de bronze.

La venue en scène, quatre ans plus tôt à Munich, de la petite Olga Korbut, aura apporté en gymnastique un tout nouveau style. L'acrobatie s'est installée maîtresse et la lignée de petits bouts de femmes inspirée par Korbut devait connaître son épanouissement à Montréal. Lorsque l'équipe féminine roumaine quitta le Village olympique, presque en sourdine bien avant le temps prévu, Nadia Comaneci avait bel et bien confirmé cette nouvelle dynastie qui devrait se continuer dans quatre ans à Moscou. Deux autres performances parfaites devaient être signées par Nelli Kim, de l'Union soviétique. Par contre, ces folles acrobaties réussies à la perfection, tant aux barres asymétriques qu'au sol, devaient du même coup signifier le chant du cygne pour celle qui fut la Grande Dame de la gymnastique jusque là, Ludmila Tourischeva, de l'URSS qui, tout comme à Mexico la Tchécoslovaque Vera Caslavska, a décidé après les Jeux de se retirer de la grande compétition. Chose certaine, même face aux succès inouïs des Comaneci, Korbut et Kim, il n'en demeure pas moins que Ludmila Tourischeva aura peut-être été la dernière dans cette dynastie chez qui la grâce, le charme, la souplesse du rythme ont permis dans le passé d'applaudir certes la gymnaste, mais avant tout la FEMME au sens complet du mot.

Si à chaque jour, un forum rempli à craquer s'accordait d'emblée aux décisions du jury devant les performances des Comaneci et Kim, il n'en a pas été de même pour les athlètes masculins. A quelques reprises, les points accordés aux performances des Japonais n'ont pas eu l'heur de plaire à la foule et les juges ont été vertement critiqués pour avoir apparemment favorisé les Soviétiques aux dépens des gymnastes du pays du soleil levant. A tel point qu'un certain soir, le président de la Fédération internationale, Arthur Gander, a quitté son siège pour se rendre auprès des juges à cause d'un pointage trop peu élevé accordé à un certain gymnaste japonais.

COURAGE INDOMPTABLE

C'est au Forum, au cours des Jeux, que le plus bel exemple de courage s'est manifesté. Le Japonais Shun Fugimoto a ressenti une très vive douleur à une jambe lors des exercices au sol. Dès cet instant, il s'est rendu compte qu'il souffrait d'une fracture de la jambe. Loin de se retirer et d'abandonner son équipe, il a accepté de se produire aux anneaux. Sa performance impeccable lui a valu la médaille d'or mais pensez un peu à cet instant dramatique alors que son tour de force terminé, il se devait d'effectuer une sortie parfaite. Retomber impeccablement sur ses pieds avec une jambe fracturée, quel effort physique et quel courage indomptable! Quelques heures plus tard, c'est un Shun Fugimoto avec un plâtre s'étendant de la hanche aux orteils mais avec une médaille d'or au cou qui souriait en affirmant combien il était heureux.

Si Nadia Comaneci a pu nettement dominer chez les dames, les compétitions de Montréal auront fait voir le renouveau soviétique chez les messieurs.

Munich ayant confirmé la supériorité japonaise même en présence d'un Nikolai Andrianov, quatre ans auront suffi pour redorer le blason soviétique. Il ne faudrait cependant pas oublier l'absence du principal espoir japonais Shigeru Kasamatsu qui a dû subir l'ablation de l'appendice à Montréal même, à quelques heures des compétitions. Puis, cette jambe fracturée dont a été victime Fugimoto n'a certes pas aidé la cause japonaise. Il serait injuste, tout de même, de ne pas souligner les performances exceptionnelles d'Andrianov dont le palmarès fait voir l'or au saut de cheval, aux anneaux et au sol, en plus de l'argent aux barres parallèles et du bronze au cheval d'arçon.

Tout comme pour Tourischeva chez les dames, c'était également le chant du cygne pour Sawao Kato, pourtant récipiendaire de quatre médailles d'or en plus d'une médaille d'argent à Munich en 1970.

A la fin des compétitions, on ne pouvait s'empêcher de penser qu'à Moscou, on devrait assister à une troisième phase du duel entre les Soviétiques et les Japonais, alors que chez ces dames, à la régression de l'Allemagne de l'Est pourrait succéder une remontée qui empêcherait un nouveau duel entre Soviétiques et Roumaines.

LA FRUSTRATION

Le simple nom d'Olga Korbut, toujours en gymnastique féminine à ces Jeux de Montréal, aura peut-être évoqué la frustration, le découragement devant l'effort ultime qui n'apporte tout de même pas le résultat espéré. L'éblouissant succès de Munich quatre ans plus tôt ne devait pas se répéter en sol canadien où, à maintes reprises, un manque d'équilibre l'a reléguée dans l'ombre d'une Nadia Comaneci et de deux de ses propres compatriotes Nelli Kim et Ludmila Tourischeva.

Tout en évoquant le nom d'Olga Korbut, cette frustration chez les athlètes a connu un tournant beaucoup plus dramatique, plus spectaculaire, aux compétitions de voile de Kingston, en Ontario. Deux marins britanniques, Alan Warren et David Hunt, devaient à leur façon dévoiler publiquement leur état d'âme dans un geste fort inusité. Alors qu'ils ont atteint l'arrivée en 14e position sur un peloton de 16 concurrents dans la catégorie Tempest, ils ont tout simplement décidé de mettre le feu à leur embarcation de fibre de verre d'une valeur de $10,000. Ce Tempest du nom de Gift 'Orse avait d'ailleurs été endommagé lors du transport à Montréal. Dégoûtés du résultat obtenu, Alan Warren a tout simplement décidé que ce bateau devait connaître une fin historique, ceci dans la plus pure tradition d'antan chez les hommes de la mer. Devant l'opaque fumée noire se dégageant de la coque de l'embarcation, les autorités canadiennes ont crû un instant à du sabotage ou à l'éclatement d'une bombe quelconque. Ainsi, dans l'espace de quelques instants à peine, toute une flottille bondée de policiers, sans oublier un hélicoptère, bourdonnait autour du Tempest abandonné à son triste sort.

SUPERCHERIE DISGRACIEUSE

L'incident le plus disgracieux de cette quinzaine demeure sans contredit la tricherie et la supercherie dont s'est rendu coupable l'escrimeur soviétique Boris Onischenko. Déjà détenteur d'un étincelant palmarès, Onischenko avait truqué son épée en y ajoutant un déclencheur manuel dissimulé dans la poignée de son arme, ce qui lui permettait en se servant du système électronique en usage de faire croire à une touche même s'il n'atteignait pas son adversaire.

Dans l'enceinte du stade d'hiver de l'Université de Montréal nul ne peut en croire ses yeux, ses oreilles . . . mais chacun doit se rendre à l'évidence. L'épée de Boris Onischenko est bel et bien truquée. Grâce à un dispositif mis au point de façon impeccable sur le plan technique, il n'a qu'à appuyer sur un bouton dissimulé sous un relief de cuir de la poignée pour que le tableau électronique enregistre une touche, sans même que l'arme effleure son rival. La supercherie est découverte lors des 16 tours aux épreuves d'escrime du pentathlon moderne alors que le Soviétique fait face au Britannique Jeremy Fox. Sur un développement par Onischenko, Fox retraite et la signalisation électronique marque une touche. Devant la plainte du Britannique, l'épée est passée au peigne fin et l'on découvre le mécanisme secret.

Ainsi, cette puissante formation soviétique, gagnante de la médaille d'argent aux Jeux de Munich en 1972 et grande favorite pour la médaille d'or à Montréal perdait du même coup la face et toute chance de triompher, subissant la disqualification officielle.

Mais qui donc est Boris Onischenko? Un athlète qui aura eu besoin de tricher dans cette discipline de l'escrime, par manque de talent peut-être? Pas du tout! Bien au contraire. Boris Onischenko, âgé de 38 ans fut médaillé d'argent à Munich aux épreuves individuelles du pentathlon moderne. A maintes reprises, il s'est assuré le championnat mondial et, plus encore, il occupe le poste de secrétaire général de la Fédération soviétique du pentathlon. Onischenko, maître émérite en sports de l'Union soviétique, a triché! Mais pourquoi? Pourquoi lui, le célèbre Onischenko, sans le moindre doute le dernier qui aurait dû recourir à une telle pratique? On ne le saura sans doute jamais mais chose certaine, la réaction soviétique officielle ne s'est pas fait attendre. Disqualifié, Onischenko a aussitôt quitté le stade de l'Université de Montréal en autobus et on ne le revit plus par la suite au Village Olympique. Toutes ses victoires, ses championnats sont maintenant rayés des manuels.

«Je ne parviens tout simplement pas à m'expliquer sa conduite car Onischenko est l'un des meilleurs escrimeurs au monde et n'avait pas du tout besoin d'utiliser une telle supercherie pour gagner.» Voilà la déclaration de M. Sandor Kerekes, directeur du pentathlon moderne aux Jeux.

REQUÊTE REFUSÉE PAR LE CIO

Le boycottage africain des Jeux a été vite relégué aux oubliettes devant les performances de Nadia Comaneci, mais il y a tout de même 684 athlètes qui, après s'être rendus sur place et s'être installés au Village, n'ont pu participer aux compétitions. Pour la première fois, du moins officiellement, l'un de ces athlètes affectés par les décisions gouvernementales, a voulu passer outre à l'ordre de ne pas se présenter aux compétitions. Le sprinter James Gilkes, de la Guyane, mais qui poursuit ses études et son entraînement à l'Université Southern California aux États-Unis, a présenté une pétition au Comité international olympique à titre de citoyen du monde et non pas à titre de porte-couleurs d'un pays en particulier, encore moins le sien. Cette requête de Gilkes a vite été rejetée par le CIO et, très amer, il a quitté Montréal en maugréant que selon lui, les Jeux avaient perdu un si grand nombre d'athlètes que le tout lui faisait penser à une simple compétition-invitation de San Diego. Remarque facile à comprendre mais tout de même totalement injuste pour tous ceux qui sont restés et qui en ont profité pour réécrire plusieurs pages d'histoire.

Ce qui n'a pas été souligné par Gilkes ou tout autre, c'est le fait que cette démission des pays africains aura signifié pour le Canada, et Montréal surtout, une perte des plus substantielles dans la vente des billets. En effet, le Comité organisateur a dû rembourser 750,000 billets déjà vendus alors que jour après jour on devait contremander des épreuves auxquelles ces pays dissidents s'étaient inscrits.

LES NAGEURS

A quelques pas du grand stade, dans une piscine merveilleuse mais autour de laquelle il aurait fallu des estrades contenant deux fois plus de sièges, on a assisté à la naissance, confirmée de façon exceptionnelle, d'une dynastie nouvelle. La puissance des nageuses de la République démocratique allemande ne laissait aucune équivoque, aucun doute sur ce nouveau type de femmes douées d'un imposant physique et d'épaules d'une puissance remarquable.

Chez ces messieurs, renouveau américain, où, même si sur le plan individuel il y a eu ce John Naber pour en quelque sorte poursuivre la tradition d'un Mark Spitz, c'est en tant qu'équipes que les nageurs des USA se sont nettement imposés. Du même coup, l'on devait noter la disparition de l'une des grandes puissances du passé tant il est devenu apparent que le déclin australien noté à Munich, exception faite de Shayne Gould, continuait à s'avérer désastreux et marquait la fin d'une étape à Montréal.

La natation, fut un assez vif désappointement pour le contingent canadien puisque, en quelque sorte, cette discipline était devenue aux yeux de tous, le sport de prédilection de nos athlètes. Certes, une récolte de huit médailles n'est pas à dédaigner mais, déplorant l'absence de médaille d'or, il faut admettre que l'obtention de deux médailles d'argent et de six de bronze ne suffit pas à redorer le blason canadien. Pourtant nos nageurs avaient pris place, avant ces Jeux, au 4e rang des puissances reconnues dans ce domaine.

Venues à Montréal, déjà en possession de 13 records mondiaux, les Allemandes de l'Est ont tout simplement prouvé, hors de tout doute, leur supériorité incontestée. Jamais dans le passé olympique, une nageuse de l'Allemagne de l'Est n'avait décroché une médaille d'or . . . mais quel revirement puisqu'elles ont quitté la piscine avec 11 triomphes en 13 épreuves et 16 des 33 médailles individuelles décernées.

Le point de mire par excellence de ce groupe d'amazones fut assurément la jolie Kornelia Ender, 17 ans seulement et blonde fiancée de son compatriote Roland Matthes, qui en 1968 et 1972, avait gagné les deux épreuves de nage sur le dos. Kornelia Ender a su glaner 4 médailles d'or, soit une de plus que toute autre nageuse dans l'histoire, ceci en plus de la médaille d'argent par équipes. Mlle Ender en a profité du même coup pour éclipser totalement sa grande rivale américaine, Shirley Babashoff, le plus bel espoir des USA. Elle s'est aussi contentée de 4 médailles d'argent avant de s'assurer, à la compétition finale, le 4 x 100 mètres relais, l'or qui lui avait toujours échappé. Mais quelle revanche pour elle que ce relais, puisque c'est aux dépens du quatuor dominé par Ender que les Américaines ont pu éviter le blanchissage.

Il y a plus encore dans les performances de Kornelia Ender, puisqu'à l'instar de John Naber chez les messieurs, elle a tenté un doublé le même jour; doublé, sans doute encore plus difficile que celui de l'Américain.

Le jeudi soir 22 juillet, en l'espace d'à peine 15 minutes, Kornelia Ender réussissait ce doublé de façon incroyable. D'abord au 100 mètres papillon, elle égalait la performance mondiale puis, remontant au départ, elle triomphait de Shirley Babashoff avec une nouvelle marque mondiale dans le 200 mètres libre. Une performance aussi étonnante que celle-là permet peut-être de souligner que le record mondial aura été égalé ou abaissé dans 22 des 26 disciplines en natation.

PARALLÈLE ENDER-NABER

Le parallèle masculin, on le trouve chez ce souriant athlète américain John Naber, 20 ans seulement, qui arborait à son cou quatre médailles d'or et une autre d'argent. Mais c'est au 100 mètres dos, que le duel tant attendu entre Naber et Roland Matthes retenait l'attention de tous. Face au record mondial de 56.3 secondes détenu par Matthes depuis quatre ans, il a d'abord abaissé ce record avec 56.19 en qualification, pour ensuite mériter l'or avec 55.49 secondes en finale. Même à cela Matthes, victime d'une intervention chirurgicale à l'appendice, d'une infection à l'oreille et d'une blessure à une épaule, a dû se contenter du bronze alors qu'un autre Américain, Peter Rocca, a terminé bon deuxième.

Le doublé Naber n'atteint peut-être pas le niveau d'effort fourni par Kornelia Ender mais, par contre, à peine une heure après avoir obtenu l'or en record mondial au 100 mètres dos, le lundi 19 juillet, ce nageur s'assure la médaille d'argent au 200 mètres nage libre, ceci après avoir terminé 8e et bon dernier en qualification. Quant aux trois autres médailles d'or, il les a récupérées dans le 200 mètres dos, aussi avec une nouvelle marque mondiale, ainsi que dans le relais.

Un seul doublé argent pour le Canada avec Cheryl Gibson, d'Edmonton, dans le 4 x 100 mètres 4 nages, devant sa compatriote Becky Smith, ainsi qu'avec l'équipe masculine de Stephen Pickell, Graham Smith, Clay Evans et Gary MacDonald, au 2e rang lors du 4 x 100 mètres 4 nages. La jeune nageuse de Halifax, Nancy Garapick, qui quelques mois avant les Jeux n'avait rien réussi qui permît d'espérer quoi que ce fût, a récolté deux bronzes. La jolie Canadienne au sourire un peu timide a terminé au 2e rang dans les 100 et 200 mètres dos. Shannon Smith a fini 3e pour le bronze dans le 100 mètres libre. Le Canada a aussi réussi le bronze au 400 mètres libre relais et 4 x 100 mètres 4 nages chez les femmes.

Peut-être est-ce une récolte assez maigre si on tient compte de l'énorme succès de l'Allemagne de l'Est ou des USA, mais quand on pense aux deux médailles d'argent et aux deux médailles de bronze obtenues à Munich, c'est le double d'il y a quatre ans. Au cours des Jeux de Montréal, les nageurs canadiens auront accumulé 8 des 11 médailles restées au pays.

TRIPLE OR POUR DIBIASI

A l'autre bout de la piscine, au tremplin, il suffit de souligner que l'excellent plongeur italien Klaus DiBiasi est devenu le premier médaillé or de haut vol à signer un triplé olympique. De Mexico à Montréal en passant par Munich, l'athlète de Bolzano, dans le nord de l'Italie, aura réussi trois performances merveilleuses en douze longues années. Ce qui nous permet, tout de même, de souligner brièvement que le succès de l'Américaine Pat McCormick aux Jeux de 1952 et 1956, alors qu'elle avait raflé les quatre médailles d'or obtenues chez les dames, tant au tremplin de 3 mètres qu'à la tour de haut vol, n'a jamais été répété.

LA COURSE À PIED

Juantorena, Viren, Jenner, Drut, Walker, Crawford, Quarrie, Moses, Beyer, Ritchter, Kazankina, Stecher, et combien d'autres encore dont les exploits au grand stade de l'athlétisme ont fait vibrer le monde, ont aussi peut-être fait oublier l'absence des Bayi, Akii-Bua et autres victimes de la politique qui n'ont pu se rendre à Montréal.

L'élégant et racé cubain Alberto Juantorena ou Lasse Viren au titre de monarque incontesté de l'athlétisme? Impossible de les départager même d'un Bruce Jenner.

Juantorena, doué d'un physique exceptionnel et d'une foulée incroyable a touché le fil d'arrivée au 400 mètres devant les Américains Fred Newhouse et Herman Frazier. Au 800 mètres, il a répété cet exploit, cette fois aux dépens du Belge Ivo Vandamme et de l'Américain Richard Wohlhuter. Mais sa souplesse, son rythme et sa foulée ont eu le don de provoquer l'exaltation de cette foule de près de 72,000 personnes.

Lasse Viren, ce Finlandais aux ressources inépuisables, semble prendre un malin plaisir à nous faire oublier la fabuleuse carrière d'Emil Zatopeck, et ses doublés tant au 5,000 qu'au 10,000 mètres. Viren, qui d'une Olympiade à l'autre, semble retomber dans l'oubli à cause de performances plus ou moins dignes de son incroyable talent, rebondit soudainement de façon saisissante pour remonter au sommet du podium. Tout comme à Munich, Viren a dominé les deux distances et, pour ajouter encore à son palmarès, s'est inscrit au lendemain du 5,000 mètres, au célèbre marathon. Ce dieu du stade a néanmoins prouvé qu'il demeurait un homme en se contentant d'une 5e position. Mais ce 5e rang avec si peu de repos le confirme facilement au titre de plus grand fondeur des dernières années, au point de se demander s'il ne tentera pas le triplé or à l'occasion des Jeux de Moscou en 1980?

Dans ce marathon, couru sous la pluie mais par temps frais, l'Américain munichois Frank Shorter a raté de justesse l'occasion de répéter l'exploit de l'Éthiopien Abebe Bikkila avec une deuxième victoire. L'Allemand de l'Est Waldemar Cierpinski, contournant en fin de course la piste du stade une deuxième fois pour ne pas risquer la disqualification, a fait voir un rythme et une cadence auxquels même Shorter a dû céder. Sa médaille d'argent ajoutée à l'or de Munich lui a permis de terminer devant Karel Lismont, de Belgique, qui pourtant dans la capitale de Bavière avait glané l'argent en s'intercalant entre Shorter et Wolde, d'Ethiopie.

C'est à Bruce Jenner que revenait la tâche d'éviter une certaine oblitération américaine au décathlon. Les Soviets Avilov et Litvinenko talonnés par le Hongrois Katus s'étaient assuré l'exclusivité de cette exténuante série de 10 épreuves il y a quatre ans. Jenner promettait la revanche américaine, revanche prévue et espérée, et il n'a certainement pas déçu. Avant les Jeux, on espérait de lui un nouveau record mondial et il s'est empressé de réussir l'exploit devant Guido Kratschmer, de l'Allemagne de l'Ouest, alors qu'Avilov, gagnant de Munich, terminait au dernier échelon du podium olympique.

Le 100 mètres a permis d'écrire une autre page d'histoire significative quant au programme américain. Pour la première fois depuis 1928, et la 2e fois seulement de toute l'histoire olympique, aucun athlète des USA n'a pu s'assurer une médaille. Haseley Crawford, de Trinidad et Tobaggo, en 10.06, a été suivi par Donald Quarrie, de la Jamaïque, et de Valery Borzov, de l'URSS, alors que l'espoir Harvey Glance a terminé au 4e rang. Borzov, grand doublé au 100 et 200 mètres de Munich, a cédé la succession du 200 mètres au Jamaïcain Donald Quarrie.

Quant à John Walker, de la Nouvelle-Zélande, son duel tant anticipé contre Filbert Bayi, de la Tanzanie, n'a jamais eu lieu à cause du départ des pays africains. Walker, avec une poussée merveilleuse à voir, aux 300 derniers mètres, a hérité de l'or suivi d'Ivo Vandamme, de Belgique, et de l'Allemand de l'Ouest, Paul Wellman. Quant à Vandamme, il ajoutait ainsi l'argent à cette autre 2e place au 800 mètres.

ATHLÈTE HUÉ

Le jeune sauteur en hauteur, l'Américain Dwight Stones, s'est amené dans la métropole canadienne à titre de grand favori pour la médaille d'or, dans cette discipline où ses principaux adversaires semblaient vouloir être des Canadiens, Greg Joy et Claude Ferragne. Dwight Stones aura eu l'honneur douteux d'avoir été le seul athlète hué par la foule pendant les compétitions. Il a commis la maladresse

de mentionner dans une déclaration qu'il haïssait les Canadiens français, qu'il ne se plaisait pas au Village olympique, que rien n'était à son goût. Ces paroles ont eu le don de soulever l'ire des Montréalais et des Québécois, à tel point que Stones est devenu la cible d'une grande partie de la foule qui l'a hué chaque fois qu'il s'est produit dans le grand stade. A la suite des qualifications, Stones s'est présenté au stade portant un chandail sur lequel on pouvait lire en lettres rouges: «I Love French Canadians». Ce genre nouveau du «Ich liebe dich» n'a pas réussi à amadouer ceux qui se trouvaient dans les gradins; peut-être étaient-ils aussi quelque peu enclins à un parti-pris bien naturel devant la présence en lice des Canadiens Greg Joy, Claude Ferragne et Claude Forget.

Lorsque le concours a repris, une pluie fine s'est mise à tomber, ce qui ne devait pas aider la cause des sauteurs. Stones, détenteur du bronze à Munich avec 2.21 m, se présentait aux Jeux en possession du record mondial de 2.31 m. A cause de son approche de côté, un style qui lui est propre, Stones a éprouvé toutes les misères du monde et il a dû se contenter de la médaille de bronze avec un envol de 2.21 m. La médaille d'argent est revenue au jeune champion canadien Greg Joy avec 2.23 m, alors que Jacek Wszola, un Polonais âgé de 19 ans, remportait la médaille d'or à la suite d'un bond de 2.25 m.

Dwight Stones qui, comme il l'avait précédemment déclaré, ne se plaisait pas au Village olympique et n'y trouvait rien à son goût a finalement plié bagage pour retourner poursuivre son entraînement en Californie.

A peine quelques jours après les Jeux, Dwight Stones en a profité pour établir une nouvelle marque mondiale avec 2.32 m, aux Jeux de Philadelphie. Ainsi, c'est tout juste si à Montréal, on a amélioré la performance de Dick Fosbury qui avait franchi 2.24 m aux Jeux de 1968 à Mexico.

L'INCROYABLE ALEXEEV

En haltérophilie, à l'aréna Saint-Michel, un amphithéâtre beaucoup trop petit d'ailleurs devant l'engouement des foules pour les performances des hommes forts, la compétition aura donné lieu à une avalanche de nouveaux records olympiques mais à très peu de nouvelles marques mondiales; quatre seulement.

Le duel entre l'Union Soviétique et la Bulgarie a donné un résultat contraire à celui de Munich où les leveurs de l'URSS triomphèrent dans l'épreuve par équipes, glanant 5 médailles d'or et 3 d'argent comparativement à 3 d'or, 2 d'argent et 3 de bronze pour les Bulgares.

Chez les mouches avec Alexandre Voronin, chez les lourds-légers avec David Rigert et l'incroyable Vassili Alexeev, les Soviétiques n'ont pas été menacés alors que le poids-lourd bulgare Valentin Khristov, âgé seulement de 20 ans, n'a eu aucune opposition réelle.

Mais c'est encore tout de même le colosse Alexeev qui,

en l'absence du détenteur du record mondial Khristo Plachkof, de Bulgarie, a montré qu'il demeurait l'homme le plus fort, inscrivant un record mondial en épaulant 255 kilos et en totalisant 970 livres. Pour Alexeev, le jeu de renouvellement constant quant à la marque mondiale, s'est tout simplement poursuivi en terre canadienne et il ne fait aucun doute qu'il continuera son ascension graduelle et graduée vers de nouveaux sommets.

C'est un Polonais, Zbigniew Kaczmarek, qui devait célébrer son 30e anniversaire de naissance en devenant le seul médaillé or à briser le monopole URSS-Bulgarie, et ce, en triomphant du Soviétique P. Korl dans les 67.5 kg.

PERTE DE VITESSE

Deux compétitions auront grandement déçu à Montréal: le cyclisme et le judo. Même face à un auditoire ne recherchant que l'occasion d'applaudir et de crier son enthousiasme devant les performances, ces deux disciplines sont demeurées ternes du début à la fin. Heureusement que le merveilleux vélodrome a connu le Tchécoslovaque Anton Tkac et l'Allemand Gregor Braun, sinon ou aurait pu se croire à des funérailles.

Comment oublier la performance d'Anton Tkac alors qu'il s'est permis de mettre un terme au palmarès fulgurant du Français Daniel Morelon dans le sprint. Par contre, ce même sprint n'a connu à peu près aucun moment palpitant si ce n'est cette toute dernière fin de course entre Tkac et Morelon. L'élimination un peu trop facile du Soviétique Sergey Kraotsov, et surtout celle du cycliste italien Giorgio Rossi, de qui on attendait beaucoup à cause de la forme physique exceptionnelle qu'il avait démontrée lors des championnats mondiaux à Montréal en 1975, ont terni cette performance.

A noter cependant les grands efforts de Gregor Braun dans la poursuite individuelle et par équipes. D'ailleurs, les épreuves de grand fond ont couronné la suprématie des cyclistes allemands avec Klaus-Jürgen Grünke (GDR) ajoutant le triomphe à l'épreuve du kilomètre contre la montre. Ce sont cependant les Soviétiques qui l'ont emporté au 100 kilomètres, et Bert Johansson, de Suède, a confirmé son brio international sur un parcours extrêmement difficile sur les flancs du Mont-Royal.

Johansson a cueilli l'or devant l'Italien Giuseppe Martinelli et le Polonais Mieczyst Nowicki. Soulignons en passant la belle tenue d'un jeune espoir canadien, Pierre Harvey, de Rimouski, au Québec, qui a su tenir le peloton pour terminer en 24e position; le plus beau succès national dans cette discipline.

Dans l'enceinte du Forum, avec ses 16,400 sièges tous occupés, la finale tant anticipée du basketball ne s'est jamais produite. Si à Munich, dans un méli-mélo indescriptible et encore aujourd'hui impossible à comprendre, les Soviétiques avaient pu profiter de la situation pour infliger une première défaite olympique à la formation américaine, c'est en demi-finale qu'ils auront baissé pavillon quatre ans plus tard. C'est aux mains des Yougoslaves, qui d'ailleurs les avaient vaincus 5 fois au préalable, que les Soviétiques ont subi l'élimination, perdant par 89-84. Entretemps, dans l'autre demi-finale, les Américains, favoris du tournoi mais alignant une équipe dont le véritable potentiel demeurait incertain, ont assuré leur participation à la finale contre les Yougoslaves en disposant du Canada par 95-75. Les Canadiens ont cependant causé la plus agréable surprise pendant tout le tournoi. Une formation sur laquelle personne ne misait et qui, tout de même, a tour à tour vaincu le Mexique, l'Australie, le Japon et surtout Cuba, médaillé de bronze à Munich. Le seul revers canadien a été essuyé face aux porte-couleurs de l'Union soviétique.

Le basketball féminin était inscrit pour la première fois de l'histoire aux Jeux olympiques. Comment penser décrocher un seul gain aux dépens des Soviétiques et de leur géante Lulinana Semenova qui depuis 1968 n'ont pas subi un seul revers en tournoi et qui forment une équipe énormément plus puissante que toutes leurs rivales? Les Américaines, avec un jeu parfois sublime, parfois erratique, se sont appropriées la médaille d'argent.

LE CAVALIER VAILLANCOURT

Sous un ciel noir et une pluis diluvienne, dans le magnifique décor de Bromont, à environ 100 kilomètres de la métropole, un jeune cavalier canadien, Michel Vaillancourt, devait célébrer son 22e anniversaire de naissance en s'assurant la médaille d'argent au Grand Prix individuel de sauts d'obstacles. Vaillancourt, en selle sur un alezan de sept ans, Branch County, n'a pas eu la tâche facile. A l'oeuvre sur un parcours fortement détrempé et des plus glissants, il l'a emporté finalement dans un barrage face à François Mathy, de Belgique, et Debbie Jauncey, de Grande-Bretagne. Fait à souligner, Michel Vaillancourt avait été le dernier membre choisi pour l'équipe canadienne, ceci après le Grand Prix de Montréal, le 27 juin, et pourtant il a été le seul du pays hôte à se distinguer en tout temps. Dans cette discipline, l'Allemand de l'Ouest Alvin Schokemoehle, avec un parcours impeccable, a accaparé l'or.

Le Canada a donc terminé ces Jeux de la XXIe Olympiade avec une fiche totalisant 11 médailles et devenant du même coup le premier pays hôte à se révéler incapable de glaner l'or une seule fois. Cette médaille d'argent de Vaillancourt, ajoutée à celle de John Wood en canoë monoplace et à celle de Greg Joy dans le saut en hauteur, ont été les seules méritées hors de la piscine.

Pour les Canadiens, une 10e place au classement par pays et un total de 108 points, c'est certainement mieux que par le passé, mais encore loin d'une performance nationale pouvant égaler le talent déployé sur le plan de la construction et de l'organisation des Jeux.

The Olympic City

Like many of the world's great cities, Montreal is built on a river. Set on an island, and circled by the mighty St. Lawrence River, the city is the gateway to a whole continent. Since its founding in 1642 by the French explorer Maisonneuve, the settlement has thrived. From its early days of Indian raids and Jesuit missions, and the turbulent era of fur traders and railway barons, Montreal in the twentieth century has become the Paris of North America. The visitor can savour the French-Canadian ambiance of the Old Town, the soaring majesty of the new, the uniqueness of the Olympic structures. The Old Town is winding streets, excellent restaurants, sidewalk cafés, and musicians in the streets. Lovingly preserved and restored, the historic section becomes a dynamic extension of the modern city and its towering skyscrapers, a scant few blocks away.

Montreal's image as a great cosmopolitan city was shown to the world by Expo 67. Now in 1976, glittering and hospitable, it has become in the eyes of the world an «Olympic City» – an honour shared with only fifteen other cities who have staged the Summer Olympic Games.

Montreal has always been a sports-minded city – the Olympic Club of Montreal had held its first «Olympic Games» there in 1844. Winters are long and brutal, and the sporting diversions Montrealers have created for themselves are many. Excellent skiing is only an hour away in either the Laurentians or the Eastern Townships. Above all, Montreal is an ice hockey city, where the Canadiens, the professional team in the National Hockey League, are looked upon as somewhere between a tradition and a religion. When Canadiens don't win the Stanley Cup, it is a dismal year and people go into mourning. When they do, the celebrations last for a week and the glow for a year.

When the snows of winter eventually depart, Montrealers turn to baseball. The only Canadian team in the American-dominated National League, the Montreal Expos command a fanatical following. Almost as devoted are the fans of the Alouettes, Montreal's professional football team in the Canadian Football League.

Montreal has always encouraged sports of all kinds. It was fitting, therefore, that it should have the distinction of hosting the Games of the XXI Olympiad. The creation of the majestic Olympic buildings has changed the face of Old Montreal. The whole character of the city's East End has been altered by the building of the Olympic Park.

Few Olympic cities carry the entire weight of staging the Games, and Montreal was no exception. A variety of satellite sites were selected to accommodate the events in sailing, shooting, equestrian, football, archery and handball.

Joliette played host to the archers, expanding to Olympic specifications one of the finest facilities for the sport in Canada. Sixty miles from Montreal, it is a quiet town on the Assomption River, in the foothills of the Laurentians.

The handball competitions were held at Quebec City. Dating back to 1535, the city was the capital of the French colony of New France and the main fortress in the wars between England and France for possession of the New World. It is a city built on two levels; the Old Town, with its narrow twisting streets huddled along the waterfront, is the original settlement, while the New Town perches high above, on the bluffs which were once the lookout posts for sentinels guarding the St. Lawrence River.

Ottawa, Toronto and Sherbrooke shared the football events. Canada's capital, Ottawa, is a pretty, tidy and compact city dominated by the Peace Tower and the Houses of Parliament poised above the broad Ottawa River. Toronto, with a population of over two millions, is the economic heartland of Ontario. In character it is far different to Montreal, holding more firmly to British ties and attitudes. It is often considered conservative by comparison to Montreal, although the influx of immigrants since the Second World War has given it a more cosmopolitan flavour. The small city of Sherbrooke is one hundred miles south of Montreal in the Eastern Townships. A flourishing industrial centre, it proved itself capable of international organization and competition by staging the World Water Skiing Championships in 1967.

L'Acadie is a suburb of Montreal, on the road to the United States border. Always the rallying point for shooters, its range was expanded and brought up to full international standards for Olympic shooting.

The sailors went further afield, to the old garrison town of Kingston, a charming city renowned for its university and the Royal Military College. Situated at the end of Lake Ontario where it flows into the St. Lawrence River, the area has long been a favourite one with those who swim and sail. Built from reclaimed land on the waterfront, the completely new facility at Kingston is one of the finest public sailing areas in the country.

Another new facility transformed the village of Bromont from a fashionable ski resort into a major equestrian site, complete with a gruelling cross-country course. Its permanent population of three thousand stoically accepted being overrun by more than fifty thousand people a day and having a royal princess in their midst.

The Olympic Events

The flame was lit, even if, in Lord Killanin's words, it was «on a lamp post instead of at the top of the stadium». The flame may have been at ground level, but on this Saturday, July 17, 1976, the Olympic Games had begun, and the eight thousand athletes would try to forget politics for the next two weeks and concentrate on what they had come for – competition. This day was, by tradition, an occasion for pomp and ceremony, for the well-dressed parade of athletes, and the setting of a mood. Not until the next day would the sweat, agony, triumph and heavy scheduling begin.

DAY TWO

The first day of actual competition saw the Soviet cyclists win the first gold medal of the Games, the 100-kilometre team time trial. They defeated Poland and a strong team from Denmark, who edged out the favoured Czechoslavakians for the bronze medal.

If cycling was unspectacular in spectator terms, the more glamorous sports such as gymnastics gave an indication of greater things to come. At the Forum, Romanian sweetheart Nadia Comaneci gave a flawless performance on the uneven parallel bars and received the first perfect score in Olympic history.

At the shooting ranges, the GDR's Uwe Potteck broke world and Olympic records in free pistol, defeating former world record-holder Harald Vollmar, with Austrian Rudolf Dolinger third. Another world record fell in weightlifting. In fact, when the flyweights finished, the Soviet's Alexander Voronin came away with a gold medal and three world records – he had not only set a new Olympic record but equalled his own world record in two lifts.

Team sports began their long grind with only a few surprises. One was in football, when late-entry Cuba held the favoured Polish team to a scoreless draw, while Brazil came away with the same result against the highly rated GDR team. In basketball, the ranked Americans, Soviets and Canadians all cruised through first-round matches without difficulty.

Activity began at the pool and also gave indication of performances to come. American Mike Bruner shattered the world record in winning the 200-metre butterfly and the GDR women set a world mark in the 400-metre medley relay. In this race the Americans narrowly defeated the Canadian quartette of Wendy Hogg, Robin Corsiglia, Susan Sloan and Anne Jardin, who won the bronze – Canada's first medal of the Games.

DAY THREE

The excitement was again in swimming and gymnastics. At the pool, three new world records were set. Kornelia Ender of GDR won the 100-metre free style and John Naber the 100-metre back stroke to establish themselves as the early superstars, and the trend of American male domination was set when Bruce Furniss took the 200-metre free style. In the 200-metre butterfly, Andrea Pollock won for the GDR.

Other medals for the day went to the Soviet women's gymnastics team which faced two more perfect performances by Nadia Comaneci. West Germany's Karlheinz Smieszek also reached a world mark in the small bore rifle, prone position, gold medal shoot. Bulgaria got into the medal lists when weightlifter Norair Nurikyan won the bantamweight gold.

Sailing began its lengthy competition at Kingston and, in team sports, a major upset appeared in field hockey when the Netherlands stunned India 3-1. Canada won merit marks in keeping the score to 2-1 while losing in football to the Soviet Union.

On the basketball courts, all matches went as predicted, but it was becoming apparent that the Soviet women's team was far ahead of all other as it toyed with Canada and won by 64 points.

In the always rugged water polo wars, the Soviet Union was pushed off balance in the hunt for a second straight Olympic gold when the Netherlands scored a 3-2 win.

DAY FOUR

For Canadians, this was a good day. Shannon Smith picked up a bronze in the 400-metre free style, joining the relay team who had also taken a bronze the day before. If Canada was taking solace, as the host country, in these two bronzes, around them in the pool world records were tumbling one after another. And the theme was familiar: American men (Brian Goodell, 1,500-metre free style, John Hencken, 100-metre backstroke) won golds and the GDR women (Petra Thumer, 400-metre free style) maintained domination.

Medal counts were building. Cycling resumed after a day off with Klaus-Jurgen Grunke, GDR, capturing the 1,000-metre time trial. The first diving medal went to American Jennifer Chandler, in springboard, and in gymnastics, the Japanese men's team – helped by a courageous display by Shun Fujimoto competing with a broken leg – emerged the all-round winners.

Donald Haldman gave the United States a clay pigeon, trap shooting, gold medal and the Soviet Union earned another weightlifting gold. This time it was featherweight Nikolai Kolesnikov.

And still the team sports waded through their schedules. This day wasn't one of anything but form. It was clear, however, that the Japanese women's volleyball team was intent on regaining the gold first won in Tokyo but not repeated since. They were steadily establishing themselves as the team to beat.

In basketball, there was almost a shocker. The United States, expecting little difficulty with a Puerto Rican team stocked with players most of whom attended U.S. universities, had to fight for a one-point win to remain unbeaten.

The first «scandal» of the Games came to light when Soviet pentathlete Boris Onischenko was sent home for cheating. It was discovered his epee was wired to record hits even though it had not actually touched his opponent.

At the rowing basin, where the competitions were still working through preliminaries and repechages, the American rowing eights failed to reach the finals for the first time in Games' history. England won the repechage with Czechoslovakia second and the Americans third and out.

DAY FIVE

The focus was again on two sports – swimming and gymnastics. At the pool, GDR female domination was broken by the Soviet Union's Marina Koshevala in the 200-metre breast stroke. That produced another world record and also saw the GDR girls blanked for the first time as two other Soviet swimmers – Marina Yurchenia and Libov Rusanova – swept the silver and bronze. Matt Vogel gave the U.S. the 100-metre butterfly and another world mark toppled when the American men churned to the 4 x 100 free style relay title. Ulrike Richter swam the GDR back to gold in the 100-metre back stroke.

In gymnastics, Nadia Comaneci, with seven perfect marks behind her, took the all-round title. Italy's 19-year-old Fabio Del Zotte fenced his way in an upset to the individual foils gold; Lanny Bassham gave the U.S. another shooting first, this time in small bore rifle, three positions, and Poland's Zbigniew Kaczmarek became the lightweight weightlifting champion.

The first meeting of unbeaten basketball teams saw the Soviets emerge unscathed, clearly out-classing a hopeful Canadian team, 108-85. The biggest upset to this point in the Games in team sports came when the Australian hockey team ran amok to humiliate India 6-1. Briefly, that

made Australia the favourite to capture the gold. For the Canadians, the only success was in swimming, where Nancy Garapick took the bronze in the 100-metre back stroke.

DAY SIX

A footnote for the Olympic history books was provided today; equestrian events began and when Princess Anne rode dressage, she became the first member of the British royal family to compete in an Olympics.

The schedule was stepping up and a flock of medals was awarded this day. Swimming was down to relays and some closeout individual events. The United States swam a world record time in the men's 4 x 100 medley relay in which Canada bagged a silver. Individually Brian Goodall took the 400-metre free style for the Americans and the great GDR swimmer Kornelia Ender added the 100-metre butterfly, equalling the world record, to her collection of wins. Just minutes later, she set a world standard in taking the 200-metre free style to cap a magnificent evening's work. Also at the pool, Philip Beggs won springboard diving for the U.S.

At the Velodrome, West German Gregor Braun captured the 4,000-metre individual pursuit in cycling and another weightlifting class was decided, middleweight honours going to Bulgaria's Yordan Mikov. The modern penthalon finished its five events and the individual winner was Poland's Janucz Pyciak-Peciak, with England's Adrian Parker, Robert Nightingale and Jeremy Fox crowned team champions.

Nelli Kim, another darling among the gymnasts, took two golds for the Soviets, winning the horse vault and then taking the floor exercise with a perfect score. Nadia Comaneci added the uneven bars and balance beam to her collection, and finished a week of breathtaking performances with an incredible score of three gold medals, one silver and one bronze.

DAY SEVEN

To many Olympic purists, this was the true start of the Games; attention would now focus upon the majestic main stadium where the track and field events were to begin. While the schedule was full in the stadium, there were only two finals. In one, Angela Voigt showed the GDR women were as strong in athletics as in the swimming pool when she took the long jump. Then, in the 20-kilometre walk, Mexican mailman Daniel Bautista won the first ever track and field gold for his country, setting a new Olympic time.

The men's gymnastics ended with Russia's Nikolai Andrianov running his medal count to seven by taking the floor exercises, rings and horse vault. Hungary's Zoltan

Magyar took side horse while Japan's Sawao Kate and Mitsuo Tsukahara won the parallel bars and horizontal bar respectively.

West German Alexander Push became the epee champion, while shooting medals went to Nobert Klaar, GDR, in rapid fire pistol and to the U.S.S.R.'s Alexandr Gazov in running game.

Another devastating win, this time over the United States 112-77, ran the Soviet women's basketball team to a 5-0 record and clinched the gold medal a game before the end of the tournament. Canada retained hopes of a medal among the men by defeating the stubborn Australians but the Americans and Soviets still remained unbeaten in their groups.

Canada's fortunes varied. In track, two of the big hopes – Abby Hoffman and Yvonne Saunders – failed to get through their heats in the 800 metres. Joan Wenzel, also ranked well, joined them on the sidelines. At Kingston, a surprise Soling crew from Halifax brought a ray of hope by winning the fourth race of the series and moved to fifth place overall in the class.

DAYS EIGHT AND NINE

With a jammed weekend schedule, the Olympics moved into their second week, and people paused briefly to check the Big Three in medal counts. The GDR had more golds (26) than the Soviet Union (25) and United States (21). In total medals, it was the Soviets (70), the U.S. (56) and the GDR (54). It was clear these three nations were the superpowers with depth in almost every sport.

At the stadium, two world records fell as Cuba's Alberto Juantorena shattered the time for 800 metres and American Ed Moses sped over the 400-metre hurdles faster than anyone in history.

Mack Wilkins of the U.S. won the discus and West Germany's Annegret Richter the prized women's 100 metres. The GDR captured two more golds; Ruth Fuchs established an Olympic record in the javelin and Udo Beyer won the shot. Trinidad's Hasely Crawford suprised all but the experts in nailing the men's 100-metre race to become what is often called the world's fastest human.

Swimming was winding down but times and performances were still up. What was viewed the biggest upset in the tank came when the American girls finally beat the GDR. That was in a world record splash to the 400-metre free style relay.

Beyond that, it was mostly form. Ulrike Tauber slashed the world record for the 400-metre individual medley and her GDR mate Hannelore Anke won the 100-metre breast stroke. David Wilkie intruded upon American male domination by winning the 200-metre breast stroke for England and John Naber added another gold, the 200-metre back stroke. Petre Thumer gave the GDR the 800-metre free

style, and Jim Montgomery set a world record in winning the 100-metre free style for the U.S. Ulrike Richter gathered another gold in the 200-metre back stroke, but in the same race, Canada's Nancy Garapick prevented an East German clean sweep by capturing the bronze. Also at the pool, Soviet Elena Vaytsekhovskala was crowned queen of the platform divers.

In the finals in women's rowing – on the program for the first time – the GDR crews won four of the six events, with Bulgaria taking the other two. The GDR also dominated the men's rowing with five gold medals. Behind them, Finland, Norway and the U.S.S.R. managed one gold each.

Cycling finished its Velodrome phase in a dramatic finale for sprint honours between four-time Olympian Daniel Morelon of France and Czechoslovakia's Anton Tkac. Tkac won out, leaving Morelon with two golds and two silvers in a career stretching back to Tokyo. The West German foursome won in 4,000-metre team pursuit.

The Soviet Union took two more weightlifting golds with light heavyweight Valery Shary and middle heavyweight David Rigert. The one fencing gold for women individual foil belonged to Hungarian Ildiko Schwarczenberger, while the men's team foil went to West Germany.

At the end of phase one of equestrian competition at Bromont, U.S. rider Edmund Coffin had won the individual three-day event. Skeet shooting honours went to Josef Panacek, Czechoslovakia.

Canada's women athletes fared well. Cheryl Gibson was second and Becky Smith third in the 400-metre individual swimming medley, giving the host country two medals in one event. Diane Jones, considered a medal possibility in the pentathlon, finished the day's competition in fourth place.

DAY TEN

Early in the day a chilly rain started to fall, creating conditions that were hardly favourable for either athletics or the gruelling 180-kilometre road race – the final event on the cycling program. After almost five hours grind, Sweden's Bernt Johansson emerged the victor, giving his country its first gold medal of the Games.

And, rain or no rain, stadium fans saw two world records and the beginning of a unique sequence of wins by Finland's Lasse Viren. The 5,000 and 10,000-metre king of Munich retained his title with an impressive win in the 10,000-metre, while Donald Quarrie of Jamaica captured the 200-metre to make the sprints an all-Caribbean preserve. The world records came when Hungary's Miklos Nemeth unloaded a gargantuan javelin toss and when the Soviet Union's Tatiana Kazankina dazzled spectators with her speed in the 800 metres. Siegrun Siegl, GDR, finished as the pentathlon queen and Poland's Tadeusz Siusarski equalled the Olympic record in the pole vault.

The first judo title went to heavyweight Sergei Novikov. In weightlifting, heavyweight Valentin Kristov won another gold for Bulgaria (its eighth).

In team sports, a startling Yugoslav basketball win over the Soviets, while the U.S. remained unbeaten, left the Americans and Yugoslavia to battle it out for the gold while the 1972 champion Soviets drew Canada to decide the bronze.

Canada's Diane Jones finished sixth in the pentathlon and Bruce Simpson and Debbie Brill failed to qualify in the pole vault and high jump respectively.

DAY ELEVEN

By Olympic standards, it was a light schedule but that did not imply a lack of either competition or drama.

In basketball, the United States regained the title lost in the controversial Munich final by crushing Yugoslavia. For the proud Americans, it was a win far beyond the gold medal.

Just as big was the gold medal performance by super heavyweight Vasili Alexeev in weightlifting. The Soviet lifter had been considered fading, with younger men ready to replace him. By the time the evening had finished, the giant had established world records and convincingly outlifted his nearest competition.

Veteran Klaus Dibiasi also earned superstar status at the pool when he took a diving gold. For the Italian, it was the third straight Olympic gold. He promptly announced he didn't intend to try for four and fans knew they had seen the exit of an artist.

Japan came up with its first judo victory when light heavyweight Kazuhiro Ninomiya fought his way to the gold. In fencing, the Soviets showed the way .in team sabre.

The long siege at Kingston finally ended. After all the compiling of the convoluted scoring, European domination was confirmed. West Germany took two golds, the GDR one and Sweden and Denmark split the other two. Canada's Flying Dutchman skipper, Hans Vogt, came close to a medal but had to be content with a fourth place.

In the football semi-finals, the GDR beat the Soviets 2-1 and Poland sidelined Brazil 2-0. In water polo, Hungary was the winner and the long-standing water war between themselves and the Soviets never had a chance to materialize. The Soviets were out of the medals completely as Hungary swam unbeaten through the tournament.

If Canada was still looking for a gold, it was able to gain solace from an unexpected silver when Michel Vaillancourt became the first Canadian in history to ride to an individual Grand Prix jumping competition. He finished behind West Germany's Alwin Schockemoehle in the competition at Bromont.

DAY TWELVE

The schedule was gathering momentum again, but it wasn't a big day for counting medals. Athletics were still primarily into preliminaries and only five finals were accomplished. However, all were interesting. France gained its first 100-metre hurdles gold in history when Guy Drut flew over the barriers ahead of the other seven finalists. Olympic records fell to Baerbel Eckert, GDR, in the 200 metres and to her mate Rosemarie Ackermann in the high jump. Sweden's Anders Garderud established a world record for the 3,000-metre steeplechase and Soviet muscle – led by Yurly Sedyh – accomplished a medal sweep in the hammer throw.

The final sailing title was decided at Kingston with Reg White and John Osborne giving England the Tornado gold. In handball, the Soviet Union clinched both male and female crowns and yet another gold went to Russia in the women's team foil in fencing. Japan continued to win in judo when Isamu Sonoda was crowned middleweight king.

In field hockey, New Zealand reached the finals by beating the Netherlands and in the other semi-final game, Australia upset favoured Pakistan. Unbelievably, it would be an all Australasian final.

For Canadians, there was bitter disappointment on the track. Veteran Grant McLaren was leading his heat of the 5,000-metres when he was jostled by two other runners. He fell, got up and finished sixth. Officials decided there was interference, disqualified the other two runners and McLaren qualified in fourth. However, later in the evening, videotapes were reviewed and the decision was reversed. The disqualifications were lifted and McLaren was back in sixth place and out. At L'Acadie, there was better news when Lucille Lemay shattered the Olympic archery record at 30 metres. Her 341 was the best score of the day, but, added to a poor start, only moved her to eighth place in overall standings at that stage.

DAY THIRTEEN

Once again, the main activity was at the Olympic stadium and the near-capacity crowd were treated to another outstanding day of athletics.

Cuba's Alberto Juantorena completed his big double as he flashed to the 400-metres finish line. Just as stunning for the crowd was Irena Szewinska. The 30-year-old Polish mother set Olympic and world records for the 400 metres and also took the third Olympic gold of her career. In all, she had competed in four Olympics and collected seven medals. GDR women continued their success. Johanna Schaller winning the 100-metre hurdles and Evelin Schlaak the best in the discus. American Arnie Robinson took the long jump.

Team Grand Prix dressage went, as expected, to West Germany but there was a gold medal upset in men's team sabre fencing when Sweden prevailed over West Germany. In judo, Soviet middleweight Vladimir Nevzorov defeated Japan for the gold medal.

By nightfall, when the Soviet Union and Brazil were clashing for the football bronze, torrential rains turned the stadium into a pond. What could have been a small classic became a slogging survival test which the Soviets finally won 2-0.

DAY FOURTEEN

This was Friday. The end was in sight but there was excellence still to come. In field events, Soviet iron man Viktor Saneev became the first man in history to win the triple jump at three Games.

The remarkable Finn, Lasse Viren also did something nobody else had done before when he repeated his Munich feat to become 5,000-metre champion. That established him as the only runner ever to win both the 5,000 and 10,000 metres in successive Games. He immediately announced he would run in the next day's marathon – his first try at the distance. Tatiana Kazankina succeeded countrywoman Ludmila Bragina as Olympic queen at 1,500 metres, keeping that crown in the Soviet Union. And the best all-round athlete was decided convincingly when the popular U.S. athlete Bruce Jenner shattered the world record for points in becoming decathlon champion.

New Zealand rounded out a hockey tournament which was upset-prone all the way by defeating the favoured Australian team. It was the first time New Zealand had ever reached the final in a major international hockey tournament. Volleyball wrapped up with Japan regaining the women's title and Poland proving the best among the men. Neither team was beaten in the Olympics.

Switzerland gained its first gold medal when Christine Stueckelberger won the individual dressage while Cuba added a judo gold to its total through lightweight Hector Rodriguez.

At the canoeing basin, the Soviets took two golds among the men and another with the women. The GDR men and women had one each while the Romanian men took the other.

At the archery ranges, the United States held sway with the arrows, with both Darrell Pace and Luann Ryan setting Olympic records.

For Canadians, it was one of those rare rewarding days. John Wood paddled to a silver medal in canoeing singles and all four relay teams in track and field earned berths in the finals.

DAY FIFTEEN

With the running of the classic relays, the gruelling marathon and the 1,500 metres, to many this day is the climax of the Olympics. This one lived up to all expectations and had the added element of steady rain to cool the marathoners and annoy field competitors.

Outside the main stadium, the final wraps were being put on a variety of sports. The Soviets won three of that day's canoeing gold medals, leaving only one each for Yugoslavia and the GDR.

In boxing, the United States and Cuba each placed six fighters in the final and, when the evening ended, the U.S. had out-titled Cuba 5-3 although Cuba had more fighting medals (8-7) than the Americans. The only golds to escape these two bitter rivals went to Poland and the GDR. Wrestling, too, had waded through all the preliminaries to finish with the Soviets on top with three golds. Japan took two, Bulgaria, South Korea and the United States one apiece.

While the rain poured on the marathoners as they did their lonely 26 miles, 385 yards, life went on at the stadium. Dwight Stones, the U.S. world champion high jumper, couldn't adjust his unusual run-up to the wet conditions and was forced to settle for the bronze, while Poland's Jacek Wszola took the gold. For Canadian fans, it was a delight to watch Greg Joy of Vancouver withstanding the pressure and staying with the Pole until the last minute to have the silver hung around his neck.

Bulgaria boasted the women's shot put queen when Ivanka Christova out-threw the opposition.

The 1,500 metres, always a highlight, brought New Zealand's John Walker to the starting line as the heavy favourite and he did not disappoint, giving a fine tactical display to win the race.

Finally, the marathoners began appearing out of the tunnel and a murmur of surprise boomed into cheering and applause as little-known Waldemar Cierpinski entered the stadium. The GDR runner, still surprised that 1972 winner Frank Shorter wasn't with him, did an extra lap just to make certain of the rules. Shorter then appeared to become silver medallist. Behind them, interest centred upon Lasse Viren and Canada's Jerome Drayton. Viren's debut at the distance was an astonishing fifth, one position ahead of Drayton in one of the few events where competitors are just as pleased with finishing as with a medal.

Finally, the relays, and they were a two-country affair. The GDR girls took both theirs and the American men ran off with both of theirs.

Judo wound up with a win for a mostly disappointed Japanese team. The home of judo finished with three gold medals – below their target – when Haruki Uemura won the open class.

On this next to last day, with the rain still falling, the big football match was the final between the GDR and Poland. A vast crowd of 71,619 – a soccer record for North America – sat in the rain to see the GDR defeat Poland 3-1.

DAY SIXTEEN

Finally the last day was here, mellow and melancholy. Six years of work and uncertainty, climaxed by the two-week sports festival, had swept up the city in a mood it hadn't known since Expo 67. Now the finale was being counted down in hours instead of days or weeks.

The Prix des Nations went into its final rounds late on a warm afternoon and horses and riders suffered in the heavy going, the souvenir of the previous night's rain. When that concluded, the team from France became the final athletes of 1976 to stand on the highest step of the medal podium.

Later that night, in the moving simplicity of the closing ceremony, the curtain fell. All those associated in the project, either as central figures or fringe players, were there: Lord Killanin, Mayor Jean Drapeau, the IOC's man in Canada, Jim Worrall, Canadian Olympic Association President Harold Wright, commissioner-general Roger Rousseau – the many, many architects in big and small ways who had created these two weeks. Then the flame was gone as 70,000 spectators lit their green chemical candles, swaying in time with the music and saying goodbye Montreal, hello Moscow.

ENVOI

In a massive program of events, many performances become lost or overshadowed by others. Two which deserve to be plucked from the broad tapestry are the decathlon and pentathlon, believed by many to establish the best male and female athletes in the world. Both events bring out all the demands: versatility, endurance, courage. Because each involves multiple events spread over two days, they build their own special pressures and that is yet another test.

American Bruce Jenner won the decathlon with a world record 8,618 points, 18 more than his pre-competition goal. In the course of competition, Jenner set personal bests in the long jump, shot put, high jump and 1,500 metres. He equalled his own best in the 110-metre hurdles and pole vault. That is reacting to pressure.

When the decathlon began, he had defending champion Nikolai Avilov as his main target with Guido Kratschmer his secondary one. The pivotal point came in the long and arduous pole vault where Jenner knew he was near the top of the class. He skipped early heights, found himself getting stale and decided to jump at 15'1¼". He missed and wondered if the rest in the cold and damp had hurt him. Jenner talked himself into throwing off doubt and made it easily. That was the turning point; the moment of doubt had passed, the trial by pressure was in the background. He finally moved ahead of everyone on the eighth event. For all intents and purposes, his gold medal was sealed. His world record was assured when he did the fastest 1,500 metres of his life for 714 points.

For the women, the five-event pentathlon demands the same endurance and in 1976 it had its own special drama, for after five diversified events, after two days, Siegrun Siegl and Christina Laser defied all the odds by finishing with precisely the same number of points, 4,745.

How close can one come to victory? It is one thing to lose a swimming race by the length of a fingernail but to battle through hurdles, shot put, high jump, long jump and 200 metres and be equal in points and have to decide medals by a rule book – that is the ultimate agony. Siegrun Siegl, who trailed her GDR team-mate by 39 points going into the final event, the 200 metres, gained 1,027 points to Christine's 988, to give them the same points. Siegl was awarded the gold because she had better performance than Laser in three of the five events.

For Canadians, the Games proved an exhilarating – and also a sobering – experience. For the first time, they were given a live exposure to the Olympics, the levels of competition, the emotionalism and the pressures under which the athletes labour. Those who criticized Canada's performances in the past, suddenly understood what all athletes are up against on this level and this huge stage.

Those who count medals, could be cynical about the lack of gold and «only» 11 silver and bronze. It appears anemic against the Soviet Union's 125, the United States' 94 and the German Democratic Republic's 90. Realistically, Canada made a good showing. The men's basketball team became the fourth in the world; the water polo team, a token four years before, made it to ninth place. Throughout the results tables, for those who wish to analyse, remarkable progress was made in most areas.

Now the ambition of those deeply involved, from athletes to administrators, is to maintain the momentum gained going into 1980. With four more years of cohesive, sensible programs, there could be far more than five silver and six bronze medals for Canada in Moscow. In that context, having the Games in Canada was the best thing that could have happened for Canadian athletes. Now people know first hand what they talked about for years – that athletes weren't simply making excuses, they were asking for help.

Die Olympiastadt Montreal

Die Bedeutung Montréals kann man schon ahnen, wenn man vom höchsten Punkt, dem Mount Royal, die 2 Millionen Einwohner zählende Stadt in der fast unendlich scheinenden Weite Quebecs vor sich liegen sieht. Über die modernen Hochhäuser der City hinweg folgt das Auge dem mächtigen St. Lorenz Strom, der irgendwo 1000 Seemeilen hinter dem Horizont in den Atlantik mündet. Der Blick erfasst aber auch das emsige Hin und Her der Menschen, die dort unten wie Ameisen dem Leben nachgehen und das Erlebnis Montréal erst komplett machen.

Hinabgestiegen ins Herz der Stadt, schlägt einem das pulsierende Leben Montréals entgegen. Man schlendert durch das elegante Westmount. Man bummelt entlang der St.Catherine Street oder schaut den mächtigen Dorchester Boulevard hinunter. In den Seitenstrassen, östlich des Boulevard St. Laurent, blickt man auf Reihen bunter Häuser mit langen, eisernen Aussentreppen. Ein bisschen Montparnasse hier und ein bisschen Fifth Avenue dort. Erst langsam sammeln sich die Eindrücke zu einem Gesamtbild: Hier ist eine Stadt, die einzigartig ist. Englische Eleganz und französische Kultur. Grosszügig und modern und doch auch altmodisch und verschnörkelt. Charmant, elegant, lässig, agil, lebensfroh, aufregend. Eine Stadt voller Gegensätze, mit über hundert Parkanlagen aber auch vernachlässigten Vierteln, an denen die Zukunft vorbeigegangen ist. Hier stehen grossartige Kirchen aus vergangenen Zeiten, stolze viktorianische Paläste und schäbige Reihenhäuser. Aber über alles dominierend sind die mächtigen Komplexe modernster Bauart: Die Kathedralen der Neuzeit. Kurz: Hier steht Montréal.

Der Seefahrer Jacques Cartier muss schon etwas besonderes an dieser Insel im St. Lorenz Strom gefunden haben, als er sie im Jahre 1535 als erster Europäer besuchte und sofort für die französische Krone annektierte. Ein Jahr vorher hatte er bereits die grosse Landfläche Ost-Kanadas ins französische Kolonialreich eingegliedert.

Erst 76 Jahre später etablierte Samuel de Champlain einen Handelsposten dort, wo die Indianer ihr Quartier Hochelaga nannten. Kurz darauf wurde er Gouverneur der Kolonie Kanada, und auf sein Betreiben florierte der Ort mit tausenden von Neuansiedlern.

Im Jahre 1642 gründete Maisonneuve die Stadt, der er den Namen Ville Marie de Montréal gab, Montréal nach dem Berg der Insel, Mont Réal, der königliche Berg.

300 Jahre nach der Gründung hatten sich fast 2 Millionen Menschen hier ein Zuhause geschaffen. Doch den Schritt zur Weltstadt machte Montréal eigentlich erst im Jahre 1960, als es sich darum bewarb, zum hundertjährigen Bestehen Kanadas im Jahre 1967, die Weltausstellung, genannt Expo 67, auszurichten.

Wie kam es dazu? 1957 hatte Bürgermeister Jean Drapeau seine Wiederwahl verloren, als er mit einem sozialen Wohnungsbauprogramm die Belange seiner Bürger befriedigen wollte. An jenem Tag, als er aus dem Rathaus auszog, entschied sich wohl die zukünftige Bedeutung der Stadt.

Drapeau, ein Mann, der keine Probleme kennt, nur Lösungen, versprach von nun an den Wählern ein bisschen mehr Utopia. «Ich hatte damals erkannt» erklärte er, als er längst wiedergewählt war, «dass die Bürger unserer Stadt, wie echte Pioniere, an einer glorreichen Zukunft interessiert sind. Für nützliche Dinge haben sie nichts übrig. Sie wollen grossartige Ruhmeshallen versprochen haben. Natürlich haben wir hier Slums, aber Slums spielen keine Rolle, wenn es gelingt, die Bürger vor prächtigen Kunstwerken staunen zu lassen.»

Mit dieser Formel hält sich Drapeau nun schon seit 16 Jahren im Amt und hat so die Stadt in zwei Jahrzehnten ins 21. Jahrhundert katapultiert.

Der Wille Drapeaus, dieses Versprechen auch in die Tat umzusetzen, hat Montréal einen frappierenden Aufstieg beschert. Er holte die Hauptsitze grosser Konzerne nach Montréal, errichtete eine grandiose Weltausstellung, für die mitten im St. Lorenz Strom eigens eine neue Insel aufgeschüttet wurde. Er baute eine neue, klassische City mit Hilfe berühmter Architekten wie Mies van der Rohe, der das gewaltige Projekt Place Ville Marie entwarf.

Drapeau legte die grosszügigste Untergrundbahn der Welt an. Er riss ganze Häuserreihen ab und baute ein imponierendes Stadtautobahnnetz. 1970 schliesslich gelang ihm der Coup de Grâce, als er in einem einzigartigen Alleingang die XXI. Olympischen Sommerspiele nach Montréal holte.

Ohne Unterstützung der Provinz Québec oder gar der Bundesregierung, fuhr Drapeau zum Kongress des Internationalen Olympischen Komitees nach Amsterdam. Während seine Hauptwidersacher von Los Angeles und Moskau mit detaillierten Hochrechnungen auftrumpften, hatte Drapeau keinerlei Zahlen zu bieten. Er sprach von billigen, sich selbstfinanzierenden Spielen. Sein einziges Argument lautete: Montréal ist eine Pionierstadt. «Wir sind in der Vergangenheit immer an der Grösse der Aufgabe gewachsen. Wir werden es auch diesmal schaffen, und Sie werden staunen.»

Jetzt galt es, plötzlich das schier Unmögliche zu schaffen. Der berühmte französische Architekt Roger Taillibert

Probleme

wurde verpflichtet ein Stadion, nein eine Ruhmeshalle, zu errichten; deren Kosten am Ende weit über die Mittel Montréals hinausgingen. Streiks, Inkompetenz, politischer Zwist, Korruption und Geldmangel stürzten das Projekt in einen Sumpf von Krisen. Die Baukosten stiegen ins Astronomische, und längst sprach niemand mehr von den sich selbstfinanzierenden Spielen.

Die Zahl der Zyniker stieg von Tag zu Tag. In einer Hysterie von Schlagzeilen jagte eine Hiobsbotschaft die andere. Bald überschritten die Kosten eine Milliarde Dollar, und am Ende des strengen Winters im Olympiajahr stand erst ein Gerippe neben dem Pie IX Boulevard, das sicherlich in wenigen Wochen kein Stadion werden konnte.

Doch Montréal war der Aufgabe gewachsen. Obwohl noch am letzten Tag Arbeiter ihre Geräte wegräumten, konnten die Olympischen Sommerspiele 1976 pünktlich am 17. Juli um 15 Uhr beginnen.

Am Vorabend der Spiele, als das «8. Weltwunder» in Glanz und Farbenpracht der Eröffnung harrte, brachte Drapeau die Scharen der Kritiker zum Schweigen als er sagte: «Nur eins hätten mir die Bürger dieser Stadt niemals verziehen: Banalität.»

Lord Killanin, Präsident des Internationalen Olympischen Komitees (IOC), hatte schon vor seiner Ankunft in Montréal den Kopf voller Sorgen. Was wird es diesmal geben? Werden politische Demonstrationen wieder am Geist der Spiele nagen? Werden die Spiele wieder zur Bühne extremer Terrorgruppen? Wird sich ein neues, noch unbekanntes Problem einschleichen?

Natürlich erwartete er Schwierigkeiten, denn noch nie war es in der Geschichte der Spiele ohne jegliche Demonstrationen gegangen. Trotzdem sprach er bei seiner Ankunft von der Hoffnung für gute Spiele, von der Zukunft und von den vielen Dingen, die noch getan werden müssten, um die Olympiade noch schöner und besser zu machen.

Er äusserte aber auch Befürchtungen, dass der Olympische Gedanke des friedlichen Messens der Kräfte, der Freude, des Fair Play und der Verständigung an politischer Kurzsichtigkeit und nationalen Interessen scheitern kann.

Schon bald stellte sich heraus, wie berechtigt seine Befürchtungen waren, als die kanadische Regierung der Delegation von Taiwan die Einreise verweigerte, weil dieses Land unter dem Namen Republik China auftreten wollte. War das dieselbe Regierung, die dem IOC versichert hatte, keine Sportler oder olympische Gruppen zu diskriminieren?

Ja, es war dieselbe. Aber solange nationale Symbole während der Spiele geduldet werden, muss man auch bedenken, inwieweit man damit in die Politik des Gastgeberlandes eingreift. Mit dem Argument, dass die Olympischen Spiele nur an eine Stadt vergeben werden, wird man sich wohl hier auf die Dauer schwer tun.

Politik hatte also die Spiele schon im Griff bevor sie begannen. Trotz einiger Konzessionen in letzter Minute, man hatte nichts mehr gegen die Flagge und die Nationalhymne einzuwenden, bestand Taiwan darauf, den Namen seiner Republik zu führen und verzichtete auf die Teilnahme.

Kaum war dieses traurige Kapitel beendet, da wehte auch schon ein starker Wind aus Afrika, der zu einem Orkan zu werden drohte. Das Gros der afrikanischen Länder wollte plötzlich den Ausschluss Neuseelands erzwingen. Wegen einer an den Haaren herbeigezogenen Lappalie. Zufällig spielte gerade eine neuseeländische Rugbymannschaft in Südafrika, und die afrikanischen Länder hatten Neuseeland als Prügelknaben ausgesucht, um ihre Opposition gegen die südafrikanische Apartheidpolitik an die grosse Glocke zu hängen.

Wo gab es eine bessere Bühne als in Montréal? Man

wunderte sich, warum der Protest nicht auch gegen Grossbritannien gerichtet war, gegen die Sowjet Union, die USA oder gar gegen Kanada. Spielten nicht zur gleichen Zeit Südafrikaner in England Tennis, auch gegen sowjetische Sportler, spielten nicht zur gleichen Zeit Süd-afrikaner in den USA Golf und spielte nicht auch gerade eine kanadische Kricketmannschaft gegen Süd-afrikaner? Aber das politische Kräftespiel, um wirksam zu sein, richtet sich immer nur gegen einen. Einen möglichstschwachen Aussenseiter.

In einer eilig zusammengerufenen Sitzung des IOC konnten die Afrikaner den Ausschluss Neuseelands allerdings nicht erzwingen. Folglich boykottierten 29 vorwiegend afrikanische Nationen die Spiele.

Man muss die Verzweiflung, die völlige Niedergeschlagenheit, die Ohnmacht der vielen Sportler aus Afrika gesehen haben, um zu verstehen, was es für sie bedeutete, als ihre Regierungen ihnen einfach befahlen, sofort nach Hause zu fahren. Seit vier Jahren hatten sie auf die Spiele gewartet, vier Jahre trainiert und auf alles andere verzichtet. Und plötzlich war alles umsonst.

Doch politische Einmischung ist nicht der einzige Faktor; die steigenden Kosten der immer gigantischer werdenden Spiele und der immer weiter um sich greifende Nationalismus, werden das IOC noch öfter als bisher zu immer neuem Nachdenken zwingen. Ein stetiger Wandel wird auch in Zukunft ein natürlicher Teil der Olympischen Spiele sein. Doch ist dies nicht ebenso ein Zeichen dafür, dass die Olympische Idee noch immer lebendig ist! Was immer Menschen tun unterliegt dem Wandel, und das Ultimo wird nie erreicht.

Auch wenn der Schatten Chinas im Raum steht und sicherlich über den Spielen 1980 in Moskau schweben wird. Wird es dem IOC gelingen die Volksrepublik China, die ein Drittel der Weltbevölkerung ausmacht, in die Olympische Familie zurückzuführen? Vielleicht hat Kanada durch seine Konfrontation mit Taiwan gar unbeabsichtigt Vorarbeit geleistet, denn wenn Taiwan weiterhin auf Verzicht besteht, steht der Neuaufnahme Chinas nichts im Wege.

Obenan unter den internen Problemen des IOC steht wohl das Verhältnis zwischen Amateur- und Berufssportler. Die Anomalität, dass kaum ein Sportler sich heute noch Medaillenchancen bei den Olympischen Spielen ausrechnen kann, ohne ein Training, dass dem eines Berufssportlers fast gleichkommt; die Anomalität, dass besonders Fussballspieler aus Ländern hinter dem eisernen Vorhang an der Weltmeisterschaft der Berufsspieler und auch am Olympischen Turnier teilnehmen; die Anomalität, dass zum Beispiel Skifahrer erst dann ins Berufslanger wechseln, wenn sie als Amateure von ihren Gönnern fallengelassen werden.

Die erst kürzlich in den USA gegründete World Sports Federation sucht eine radikale Änderung auf diesem Gebiet. Sie sucht eine völlig offene Olympiade mit der Begründung, dass niemand schneller laufen kann als ihn seine Beine tragen, bezahlt oder nicht bezahlt. Auch argumentiert sie, dass ein Berufsgolfer keine Vorteile haben kann, wenn er olympisch segeln will, oder ein Berufsspieler im Baseball, der olympisch rudern will.

Viele andere Punkte stehen aus und werden die Diskussionen nicht einschlafen lassen. Neue Ideen werden sich herauskristallisieren. Vielleicht werden die Spiele unter mehreren Olympiastädten rotieren. Einige Städte bieten sich da mit kompletten und modernen Anlagen an.

Vielleicht werden Sportarten, die sich auf das menschliche Urteil verlassen, wie Turnen oder Säbelfechten, von einer Gruppe neutraler Richter aus nicht beteiligten Ländern beurteilt. Das würde sicherlich heute existierende nationale Einflüsse reduzieren. Vielleicht werden auch Hallensportarten während der Winterspiele abgehalten, um die Übervölkerung der Olympischen Dörfer im Sommer zu drosseln. Besonders, wenn mehr und mehr Mannschaftssportarten zugelassen werden. In Montréal wurde Handball und Rudern zum ersten Mal auch für Frauen ausgetragen, und in Moskau kommt Feldhockey dazu.

Über eins waren sich die Sportler in Montréal einig, obwohl Dutzende von Fahnenstangen nackt dastanden und ihren afrikanischen Fahnen nachzutrauern schienen: Die Spiele werden überleben. Sie sind ein wichtiges Instrument echter internationaler Zusammenarbeit. Wären sie nicht da, müsste man sie wahrscheinlich erfinden. Sie sind nicht perfekt. Aber sie sind besser, weitaus besser, als die einzige Alternative: Keine Spiele.

So wurde auch in Montréal die Flamme der Verständigung weiter geschürt. Menschen aller Herren Länder fuhren nach Hause und trugen Erinnerungen mit sich, die ein Leben lang ein freudiges Andenken sein werden. So war Montréal ein Weg in die Zukunft.

La Citta Olimpica

La fiamma di Olimpia approda nella terra dei Castori e delle Giubbe Rosse. L'accoglie Montreal saldamente ancorata sul St. Lawrence River. Sul fiume la citta' ha edificato le sue fortune, le sue diramazioni tentacolari. La primitiva isola abitata dagli Iroquois, gelosi custodi del passaggio a nord-ovest, é ora un mosaico di verde e cemento. I moli e la stazione centrale non pullulano piu' di passi incerti, di volti timidi di giovani emigranti. Nell'era dei jets e della discesa su Marte, Dorval e Mirabel sono i porti della nuova frontiera. Anche l'immigrazione é diversa: il giovane con la valigia serrata da lacere corde é un ricordo remoto. Oggi é di moda l'uomo d'affari, armato di «ventiquattrore», che attraversa l'oceano per piazzare i suoi capitali. La citta' si presta al gioco per cui l'America é dietro ... l'angolo, Montreal «europea» soprattutto per volere del sindaco.

UN SINDACO COCCIUTO

E' Jean Drapeau. Dagli anni '50 tiene in mano le sorti dei Montrealesi. Non despota, bensi' tiranno illuminato. Scopre i Giochi casualmente, e se ne innamora. Non a caso, comunque, confina la sua citta' in una dimensione internazionale di ampio respiro. Gia' l'Esposizione Mondiale del 1967 richiama a Montreal milioni di visitatori. E' storia recente, questa. La leggenda potrebbe incominciare con l'ingresso della fiaccola olimpica nello stadio da ottocento milioni di dollari. E' nella costruzione degli impianti che la citta' ha sostenuto gli sforzi maggiori. L'ansia e il dubbio di non farcela hanno contraddistinto una vigilia vissuta in un fiume di calcoli, di alchimie e auto-finanziamenti. L'intervento del Governo Provinciale dissipa le incertezze; i Giochi e il prestigio del Quebec sono salvi. Montreal é pronta ad accogliere la gioventu' mondiale, a vivere la bellisisma favola olimpica.

ARRIVANO GLI OSPITI

I preparativi si svolgono all'insegna della squisita ospitalita'. Fini ai minimi particolari. Oltretutto, arriva Sua Maestra', Elisabetta II d'Inghilterra, a dichiarare aperti i Giochi. Ma sopratutto arrivano gli ospiti. Tanti ospiti da ogni parte del mondo: Montreal si offre nitida e fresca. Ora, in tempi di festa, ovunque fioriscono bandiere: la foglia d'acero, il giglio quebecchese, i cinque anelli. Rosso, bianco, azzurro e il verde dei prati sono i colori di una citta' che sente la portata di avventimenti irripetibili. Il «marchio» olimpico sventola sui piu' alti pennoni, distingue i prodotti delle ditte «sponsors»: le Olimpiadi sono anche un affare economico. L'abbellimento della citta', in verita', é una filosofia. I cartelli che indirizzano ai luoghi delle competizioni sono in armonia con l'ambiente circostante, adempiono adeguatamante alla loro funzione. Non ci si puo' sbagliare ne' perdere. Montreal, del resto, é una citta' «squadrata». Basta conoscere i punti cardinali e si dispone di un patrimonio immenso ... «Handle it with care» – é solo un prestito!

I MONTREALESI

In ogni caso intervengono le hostess. Alcune in motoretta scorazzano per le principali arterie cittadine. Si avvicinano con un sorisso e soccorrono il turista distratto o in panne. Al Villaggio, allo stadio, al Forum la divisa rossa le rende inconfondibili. Di ogni razza e costume, parlano alemo tre lingue, alcune anche cinque: per merito loro é caduta anche quella distinzione manichea tra anglofoni e francofoni. In favore del Quebec, del Canada, sotto la bandiera olimpica. I due terzi della popolazione (3 milioni circa) risalgono al ceppo francese, a quel Jacques Cartier scopritore e colonizzatore del Quebec. L'anima economica, pero', é inglese, o meglio americana. Accanto ad essi i gruppi etnici adottivi. Da qui un tratto cosmopolita che sfocia in conflitti culturali e linguistici codificati persino da leggi. L'ospite comunque viene assorbito dalla spontaneita' e dalla immediatezza della citta'. Downtown, St. Catherine Street, Place Ville Marie, Vieux Montréal, St. Joseph Oratory, il fiume, e il Mont-Royal – il locale Olimpo degli Dei – che dai suoi 210 metri d'altezza sfida i grattacieli sottostanti e abbraccia a vista d'occhio l'intera citta'. D'autunno poi si tinge di mille colori. L'inverno é lungo, rigido. Il mondo sotterraneo della metropolitana con boutiques, cinema, grandi magazzini e pubs consente una liberta' di movimenti altrimenti limitata dai rigori del clima. Un sorso di whisky, un week-end in montagna a sciare, ed é subito primavera ....

LA PAURA

Il Villaggio Olimpico, nella parte est della citta', é circondato da una rete metallica alta tre metri. Le Giubbe Rosse fanno buona guardia agli ingressi: Sui tetti sono appollaiati i paracadutisti dell'esercito in tuta mimetica. Da combattimento. Chi varca i cancelli deve sottostare ad un cerimoniale non sempre simpatico. Esibire credenziali, depositare borse, sottoporsi ad accurate perquisizioni

anche elettroniche. Nel cielo, il costante ronzio degli eli-
cotteri militari: sono le sentinelle alate dei Giochi. La pre-
parazione delle truppe é stata meticolosa, sofisticata, co-
stosa. Qualcosa come cento milioni di dollari: circa
diecimila dollari per ogni atleta. Una squadra «Alfa» ad-
destrata all'antiterrorismo è il fiore all'occhiello di un di-
spositivo di sicurezza che impiega oltre sedicimila unità.
Dopo il «raid» di Entebbe, i palestinesi hanno promesso
una risposta spettacolare. Lo scenario olimpico è altret-
tanto spettacolare ed allettante. Bisogna stare all'erta.
Montreal paga lo «scotto» di Monaco e la paura incombe
sui Giochi.

ALTRE SEDI DELLE COMPETIZIONI

Kingston è il porto della flotta olimpica. Si lascia il Quèbec
per l'Ontario. Forse è un'altra terra, un altro paesaggio ma
è sempre il verde il colore dominante. Sulle acque del lago
Ontario, immenso, gli atleti affidano le vele ai venti e
«pescano» l'alloro olimpico. Toronto, Ottawa – capitale
del Canada – Quebec City, Bromont, L'Acadie, Sherbrooke, e Joliette. Ogni città vivrà un capitolo della lunga
favola olimpica. Il conto, però, va solo a Montreal e al
Quebec.

And so it begins» – annuncia biblica-
mente la stampa locale. Nel tempio dell'architetto Taillibert, dinanzi alla regina d'Inghilterra e ad una folla di oltre
73 mila spettatori. E' il primo record. Mai nella storia di
questo Paese, tanta gente é stata convocata dal richiamo
di un evento di qualsiasi natura.

L'ATLETA E IL COMPUTER

E' partita, dunque. Pur tra le immancabili polemiche,
puntuale e precisa come tutti gli impianti elettronici che
valuteranno le prestazioni degli atleti. I cronometraggi
manuali possono anche fallire, quelli elettronici no. Per
l'atletica, addirittura sono previsti tre impianti: impossibile
incappare in errori anche in caso di guasti. S'incomincio' a
Tokio con l'elettronica al servizio dello sport. Poi attraverso Messico, Monaco e il «Golim». Oramai nulla viene
lasciato al caso. I Giochi sono paragonabili ad una spedi-
zione Apollo, dove gli astronauti fungono da atleti. I cer-
velli elettronici si sostituiscono a tutto e forse un giorno
non lontano a tutti. Fra quelli che non hanno bisogno di
pensare scopriamo il «sioux» Pace. Un diciannovenne americano del viso punteggiato dalle lentiggini: centra l'oro
nel tiro con l'arco. L'arciere infallibile ha affidato ad un
computer il compito di calcolare la velocita' ottimale delle
frecce da lanciare dai 90 metri e successivamente da 70, 50
e 30 metri.

In questo esordio, solo i giornalisti sono costretti a pensare per poter coordinare le immagini visive ed uditive. Il
progresso ci ha portati verto la disumanizzazione? Certa-
mente. L'era dei robot, tuttavia, ha raggiunto lo zenit. E se
i corsi e ricorsi storici non sono soltanto un'invenzione
filosofica dovremmo entrare presto nella fase discendente.

SARA' LA SALVEZZA?

Da questo agglomerato di elettronica, balistica, trigono-
metria e idrodinamica spunta fuori una bambina rumena
che manda a catafascio tutto un sistema. Con Nadia Comaneci, appena quattordicenne, i tabelloni elettronici entrano in crisi: non . . . reggono al punteggio «dieci» che
non é previsto nei calcolatori. Sara' il pubblico mont-
realese del Forum a conferire la lode e il bacio
«accedemico», tanti baci per la verita', a questa ragazzina
che ha fatto della ginnastica una melodia di gesti e figure
motorie. «La dea con lo squardo di brace» l'hanno chia-
mata subito ed hanno pagato anche 200 dollari per veder-
la. Il Forum non é piu' il tempio dell'hockey, qui sport nazionale. Maurice Richard, il grande Jean Beliveau e tanti
altri come se non fossero esistiti. La' dentro si parla un al-

tro linguaggio. Un collega che ha avuto modo di seguire la Nadia molto da vicino dice che alle parallele asimmetriche ha dimostrato la «grazia e la femminilita' di una parigina e l'estrosita' di una scimmietta sui rami di un albero». In questa atmosfera le sette medaglie (quattro oro, due argento e un bronzo) di Andrianov passano quasi inosservate. Eppure il russo ha fatto meglio della piccola bambola rumena: cinque medaglie della quali tre d'oro, una d'argento e bronzo.

Intanto arriva il saluto papale: «Festa della gioventu' e motivo di riconciliazione e concordia tra tutti gli uomini»: é la definizione che la Santa Sede da' a questi Giochi. I giornalisti tutti presi a sbrigare «pass» speciali fanno fatica a dare la caccia al personaggio. La fitta rete di protezione che gravita sui Giochi non lascia spazio. Talvolta é difficile circolare liberamente persino con la carta di accreditazione. Gli atleti sono sorvegliati a vista. Forse é necessario: il ricordo di Monaco ci tormentera' fino alla chiusura. I Giochi scendono in strada con i quartetti della «cento»: il ciclismo ha un largo seguito qui. Il percorso é stato tracciato sui rettilinei di un'autostrada. Si corre contro vento e per il quartetto sovietico é medaglia d'oro. In pista, il francese Claude Morelon manca il «poker» e deve accontentarsi dell'argento nella prova di velocita'. L'oro va al cecoslovacco Tkac.

CROLLANO I MITI

Nella piscina olimpica entrano in acqua i «sottomarini». Per le fanciulle – si fa per dire – della Germania-est, sono subito records. Alla fine saranno ventinove solo quelli mondiali. Sono donne? Secondo i risultati del «sex control» non ci sono dubbi: 1200 ragazze sottoposte al test (analisi della saliva e degli ormoni) sono tutte donne. E' un . . . rito antipatico ma necessario. Non si sa mai . . . Comunque, amazzoni e veliste sono esentate da questa prova preliminare: si battono contro gli uomini. Ineccepibile il servizio di assistenza santaria. Naturalmente non mancano profilattici e anticoncezionali. Il dott. Letourneau, direttore sanitario del Centro, dichiara: «Non abbiamo idea di quanti ne verranno utilizzati, ma siamo in grado di soddisfare qualsiasi richiesta». Quest'anno, poi, le atlete possono accedere agli alloggi degli atleti . . . Ma torniamo in piscina. Alla leadership delle donne tedesche orientali (11 medaglie d'oro; le briciole vanno alla russa Koschevaia nella «rana» e alla staffetta 4 per 100 stile libero che salva l'onore yankee) fa eco quella americana nel campo maschile. Vincono infatti dodici finali su tredici. Si contano le bracciate 58, no 55, come si misurano i battiti cardiaci. E' un nuoto di altre epoche che si esprime compiutamente in Jim Montgomery. Vince in 49"99 i cento metri stile libero frantumando il muro dei 50" ritenuto invalicabile. Un altro mito é crollato dopo che John Wiessmuller cinquantaquattro anni fa aveva nuotato la stessa distanza in meno di un minuto. L'attuale distanza tra «Tarzan» e Montgomery é quasi di mezza vasca. Fra altri cinquant'anni l'impresa storica di Montgomery sara' ridicolizzata. John Naber l'ha imitato nei 200 dorso: battuto Matthes nel tempo record di 1'59"19. Non é stato un fatto occasionale. Naber ottiene due medaglie d'oro e una d'argento nelle prove individuali e due primi posti nelle staffette: cinque medaglie per un bottino lusinghiero. Ma siamo ancora lontani dalle sette medaglie d'oro di Monaco di Mark Spitz.

ENDER «ÜBERALLEN»

Ed ecco spuntare la sirena Kornelia Ender: quattro medaglie d'oro ed una d'argento, condite da una miriade di records mondiali. La tedesca dell'est é sempre pronta a distribuire sorrisi e baci ed é anche belloccia malgrado possegga un collo taurino e spalle da lottatore. E' riuscita a distruggere nel giro di poche ore i miti delle Fraser e della Gould che sembravano insuperabili. A questi Giochi prendono parte anche i canadesi che hanno modo di mettersi in evidenza nello scontro tra i giganti della piscina. Ne escono a testa alto: contro americani, sovietici e tedeschi, qualsiasi impresa si colora di titanismo. Ed ancora le donne fanno la parte delle leonesse. Le ondine infatti conquistano sette medaglie su otto: un vero successo, meglio che a Monaco. Gail Amundrud, Barbara Clark, Wendy Cook, Becky Smyth, Anne Jardin e le altre di dividono bronzo e argento, gioia e lacrime. A conclusione delle gare di nuoto festeggiano con qualche sorso di champagne le loro «vittorie». Alcune sono espulse dal Villaggio.

I Giochi si son mossi lentamente; dopo i primi timidi passi ora corrono: sono vivi e continuano il loro cammino tra una folla che rivela un interesse impensabile. Gli osanna al sindaco Drapeau che ha imposto i Giochi alla citta' raggiungono toni elegiaci. L'atmosfera comunque é sempre inquinata dall'annuncio che i terroristi sono alle porte. Nessun panico per questo Annibale della nostra generazione. Entebbe ha dimostrato che i terroristi possono essere battuti. I Giochi non hanno nulla da temere. Al Palazzo dello Sport di Sherbrooke viene annunciata una bomba di imprecisato potenziale: si é appena concluso l'incontro di pallamano tra Giappone e Jugoslavia. Gli agenti di sicurezza trovano in una toilette una scatola da cui partono due fili collegati al meccanismo di chiusura della porta; falso allarme: é solo una sveglia. I fomentatori del terrorismo sono sempre in agguato ma i Giochi cercano di ignorarli.

SCANDALO AI GIOCHI

Al terzo giorno di gare i Giochi vivono il loro . . . «scandalo al sole» in virtu' dei trucchi del sovietico Boros Onistchenko durante la prova di scherma del pentathlon moderno contro l'inglese Jeremy Fox. Il russo invertendo i fili che collegano la sua arma all'apparecchio segnalatore e installando nell'impugnatura un interruttore riesce ad «influenzare» il sistema elettronico che segnala le stoccata, senza toccare l'avversario. Protesta ovviamente l'inglese quando la spia luminosa gli addebita una stoccata senza essere stato minimamente «toccato» dall'arma del sovietico. L'imbarazzo e le proteste dei tecnici sovietici, apparentemente ignari dell'inganno, non impediscono la squalifica dell'atleta. E' solo un episodio che comunque pone un interrogativo non troppo irreale: e se qualcuno un giorno riuscisse a comandare a distanza l'intero sistema elettronico? Allo «stade d'hiver» dell'Universita' di Montreal inizia l'affollatissimo torneo di fioretto maschile. L'Italia conquista la sua prima medaglia d'oro con un diciannovenne veneziano dalla stoccata facile. E' Fabio Dal Zotto che manda in tripudio il clan degli schermitori azzurri e lascia di stucco gli avversari con una tecnica schermistica che non ha nulla a che vedere con i canoni tradizionali. Al bacino olimpico scendono in acqua le prime inbarcazioni. Da Kingston giungono notizie che la «flotta olimpica» ha tolto gli ormeggi malgrado le tempeste. Entra in scena l'atletica. L'Olimpiade é viva. Lo sport o meglio gli atleti stanno vincendo la loro battaglia contro la politicizzazione. Il pubblico «scopre», finalmente, i Giochi. I giornalisti percorrono delle vere e proprie maratone giornaliere. Il tempo é tiranno, i fusi orari delle vere spade di Damocle. Il centro stampa principale é al ventiseiesimo piano della torre sud di Place Desjardin. Nei momenti piu' critici viene il desiderio di lanciarsi a «volo d'angelo» e planare su un campo di . . . cemento. Per i piu' la giornata lavorativa finisce alle cinque del mattino e ricomincia alle dieci. Compagne fedeli, sempre con il sorriso sulle labbra, le hostess.

NEL TEMPIO DEGLI ATLETI

Finalmente ritorniamo nel grande stadio lasciato il giorno dell'inaugurazione. Il pubblico scopre subito due idoli. Il messicano Colin Bautista é la prima medaglia d'oro dell'atletica. Dopo venti chilometri di marcia attraverso i viali del Giardino Botanico si presenta tutto solo nello stadio. Affronta il giro di pista in scioltezza e conclude in un tempo record. Come «ouverture» non c'é proprio che dire. Bautista é una di quelle «piante» messicane con sangue indio. Per questa razza la fatica é un fatto di vita. La sua vittoria é il naturale premio a tanti anni di lavoro in profondita' della federazione messicana in questa specialita'. Lavoro sfibrante sulla quota di 2400 metri di Citta' del Messico e dei 4500 delle montagne che portano verso Puebla. Al tramonto giunge il guerriero della pista: il cubano Alberto Juantorena. Fortissimo nei 400 non nasconde le sue ambizioni negli 800 scoperti casualmente solo di recente. Con la sua agile e possente falcata percorre i due giri di pista nel tempo record di 1' 43"5 mandando in delirio i settantamila del tempio e coronandosi idolo della folla. Ancora qualche giorno e mette in fila die-

tro le sue solidissime spalle il terzetto dei quattrocentisti americani, capitanati dal grande Federick Newhouse. Popo una distratta partenza il cubano stronca con la sua forza – perché questi 400 li ha vinti di forza oltre che con la volonta' – le ultime speranze degli americani. Per Newhouse medaglia d'argento il sogno della vittoria finisce pochi metri prima del traguardo. Non é record, ma la miglior prestazione al livello del mare: 44"26. I tecnici parlano di rivoluzione storica: un quattrocentista infatti non aveva mai vinto anche gli 800 metri. Ritorna alla mente Harbirg. Non c'é confronto. Il primato degli 800 apparteneva ad un'altro quattrocentista: Marcello Fiasconaro che aveva fatto segnare 1'43"70 nel giugno 1973. Ma l'oriundo italiano non ha avuto fortuna con i Giochi: i tendini gli hanno tarpato le ali sia a Monaco che a Montreal. Dal mazzo dei giavellottisti esce un ungherese figlio d'arte che fa volare l'attrezzo a metri 94, 58 al primo lancio. Miklos Nemeth di Budapest dove é nato il 23 ottobre 1946 é il nuovo primatista del mondo l'urlo unanime della folla lo commuove: salta dalla gioia. Non crede ai suoi occhi. Guarda e riguarda il tabellone elettronico che segna il nuovo primato mondiale. Rinuncia ai due lancia successivi: l'emozione non gli consente neppure d'impugnare l'attrezzo. Gli altri, colmi di ammirazione, ma rassegnati, continuano a lanciare per colpire l'argento o il bronzo. Delude il sovietico Sidlo grande favorito. A L'Acadie, nella ventosa «fossa» del tiro a volo l'americano Haldeman trova l'alloro olimpico, mentre la pistola del tedesco orientale Pottek centra l'oro.

FINE DI UN'ERA

Per Giorgio Cagnotto ancora tuffi d'argento dal trampolino. «Per me a ventinove anni – ha dichiarato dopo la gara – questa medaglia vale quanto quella d'oro. Boggs era imbattibile». Da Tokio a Montreal, quasi quindici anni di capocciate nell'acqua. Quattro Olimpiadi lasciano il segno di una maturita' non solo sportiva. Ora l'aspettano i giovani. In campo femminile, oro per l'americana Chandler dal trampolino. Soltanto seconda la svedese Knabe (battuta dalla russa Vaytsekhoskaia) dalla piattaforma. Ma il re é solo lui: Klaus Dibiasi alla terza medaglia d'oro consecutiva. L'americano Louganis, appena sedicenne é ottimo secondo. Con lui si riaprira' un'era, perché quella Dibiasi si é conclusa con l'ultimo tuffo che gli ha dato anche la lode: nel punteggio infatti spiccava anche un dieci. Una vera apoteosi per il piu' grande tuffatore di ogni epoca.

SUA MAESTA' . . .

Valeri Borzov cede lo scettro di re dello sprint al trinideno Haseley Crawford, 26 anni e un amaro ricordo delle Olimpiadi di Monaco dove dovette ritirarsi nella finale dei 100 metri perché infortunato. Don Quarrie é secondo davanti al campione in carica Borzov. La RDT continua la sua dittatura anche nell'atletica vincendo il giavellotto femminile con Ritha Fucs e il peso maschile con Udo Beyer. La sovietica Kazankina vince gli 800 metri nel tempo record di 1′54″94, continuando alla distanza il duello con le atlete tedesche orientali. Il giamaicano Don Quarrie vince la prova dei 200 metri; Mennea é quarto, primo degli europei e dei bianchi. I lampi neri dei Caraibi, quindi, sfrecciano davanti agli americani nello sprint. Gli USA colgono l'oro dei 400 ad ostacoli con Moses, regolare con tredici falcate fra una barriera e l'altra: ferma i cronometri a 47″64. Il record precedente apparteneva ad un'altro negro, africano pero', Akij Bua sceso dal treno olimpico assieme agli altri africani subito dopo la partenza. In una giornata ricca di emozioni, la tedesca federale Richter corre, in semifinale, i più bei 100 metri della storia dell'atletica femminile: 11″01. L'oro olimpico non le sfugge a discapito della mortificata bicampionessa di Monaco Renate Stecher. Siamo quasi all'epilogo. Il «regno» di Bromont é ancora scioccato dalla principessa che cade da cavallo. Sembra proprio finita l'era d'oro dei colonnelli italiani.

Il torneo di pugilato, con i verdetti non sempre oggettivi, é una questione fra cubani e americani «colored». Spiccano su tutti due nomi: l'americano Leonard e il cubano Stevenson.

Nella pallavolo i polacchi superano i russi in un finale oltre che da cardiopalma da manuale. La lotta greco-romana é una questione prettamente sovietica; quella «libera» un po' meno per l'intrusione di qualche giapponese come Takata e qualche coreano ficcanaso.

Non sono mancati i risvolti umoristici. Mike Farina, baldanzosa lottatore americano, sale sulla bilancia per il controllo del peso ma l'apparecchiatura elettronica segnala una eccedenza di peso. Mike si toglie gli occhiali ma il segnale rosso non si spegne. Allora sputa il chewing-gum e la spia gli da' il benestare per la competizione. Dopo pochi minuti é eliminato dal russo Lexei Schmakov che giustizia sommariamente le ultime speranze olimpiche di Farina.

Nell'hockey sul prato il Pakistan arriva appena al bronzo. Alla rivelazione Nuova Zelanda l'oro seguita dall'Australia. Canottaggio, canoa sollevamento pesi appartengono esclusivamente ai Paesi dell'est europeo.

A Kingston le vele svedesi, inglesi, danesi e tedesche si fregiano d'oro. Gli altri? Li hanno visti alla deriva.

IN LONTANANZA, I TAMBURI ...

Ti viene voglia di andartene a spasso per le strade di Montreal, dove é in atto un'olimpiade dell'arte e della cultura. Ma l'alienazione atletica ti inchioda ancora una volta sulla tribuna stampa dello stadio dove la Szewinska percorre un'orbita «extra terrestre» in 49″29: record mondiale dei 400. Il neozelandese Walker atleta dell'anno nel'75 piomba come un falco biondo sul traguardo dei 1500.

Vandamme, come negli 800, é ancora secondo. Lasse Viren, l'uomo delle betulle, dopo aver seguito Sousa Lopes su un ritomo infernale negli ultimi cinque chilometri (13′32″) se ne va tutto solo verso il traguardo – dei 10000 metri – nell'ultimo giro di pista. Il finlandese vince anche i 5000 metri. Due olimpiadi per quattro medaglie. Victor Saneiev vienne dal Mar Nero ed é «professore» di salto triplo. Alla quinta prova azzittisce l'americano Butts atterrando a metri 17,29.E' la sua terza medaglia d'oro consecutiva. E' approdato all'atletica nel 1963. Recordman d'Europa ed ex primatista del mondo, Saneiev ha dedicato la sua giovinezza a questo gioco del «canguro». Quest'altra medaglia é il premio alla sua serieta' e al miglioramento tecnico che ha iniettato a questa specialita'.

Nel salto in alto in un'atmosfera da «baruffe chiozzotte» tra il primatista del mondo Stones e il pubblico s'inserisce il polacco Wszola che vince saltando metri 2,25. Il Canada finalmente conquista la sua prima e ultima medaglia nell'atletica con Joy che toglie l'argento a Stones. Un pomeriggio che i canadesi non dimenticheranno mai. Le immagini di questi Giochi sono infinite e vengono alla mente aggrovigliandosi una dietro l'altra. Dipanare la matassa non é facile anche perché lo spazio é il nostro tiranno. Si sentono già i tamburi degli indiani in marcia verso lo stadio olimpico.

LA GRANDE CORSA

Ed é quasi al suo epilogo, nell'ora somma dell'Olimpiade che entra nello stadio un Filippide sconosciuto. Indossa, inzuppatissima di pioggia e quasi impastata con la propria pelle, la maglia della Germania-est. Proprio quando il tedesco s'affaccia sulla pista echeggiano nella «bomboniera» di Montreal le note dell'inno della DDR per le cannazionali della 4 per 400. La piccola Germania, grandissima nello sport, vive il suo momento piu' significativo di un'Olimpiade ricca e sontuosa. Il maratoneta che é entrato in pista per primo si chiama Wardemar Cierpinski, ha ventisei anni e un figlio di nome Andrea. Viene dai 3000 siepi con risultati modesti. La calma e sobrieta' dei colleghi e dei tecnici della Germania-est svanisce in questa circonstanza. Si precipitano nel ricovero dei maratoneti e uno di loro rischia addirittura di farsi arrestare valicando le transenne. Wardemar, non del tutto esausto, si avvicina ai suoi amici: l'atmosfera é quasi allucinante. E' vero che questa corsa ha finito da tempo di essere un evento piu' umano che tecnico; é vero che con l'avvento di taluni fuoriclasse della pista ha trovato una dimensione tutt'altro che coloristica. La fatica tuttavia non perdona nessuno e lascia una maschera sui volti di tutti. Anche Shorter medaglia d'oro a Monaco, bellissimo in corsa sembra un derelitto. E non parliamo dell'altro americano Rodgers che pare un fuscello che crolla al primo soffio di vento. Una tazza di té, un massaggio, una coperta, tre o quattro infermiere-poliziotte che si adoperano per rianimare i piu' provati.

Ecco Lasse Viren: é arrivato quinto, ma cotto. Vi é anche il canadese Jerone Drayton. Ha stretto i denti per arrivare con i primi, anche se con passo penoso. Compare anche Fava, uno scheletrino vestito di pelle. E' il piu' giovane del gruppo ma ottimo ciociaro alla «battaglia di Maratona». Davanti a settantaduemila spettatori i calciatori tedesco-orientali riassumono la felicissima stagione olimpica. Battono nettamente i polacchi per 3 a 1, in una lunga notte, preludio della fine.

PENTATHLON E DECATHLON

L'espressione della magiore capacita' motoria e la grazia della donna, la forza dell'uomo nel contesto di una superiorita' che trova le sue origini nell'era della pietra, sono il contenuto delle prove di pentathlon e decathlon. Le cinque prove femminili e le dieci maschili non sono altro che le fatiche di Ercole nell'era moderna. Queste due competizioni ci propongono in chiave sintetica tutto il capitolo dell'atletica. In trentasei ore di magnifica lotta, gli atleti chiusi nel proprio silenzio e soli contro i cronometri e le cordelle metriche, danno vita ad un rito che rasenta i limiti dell'irreale. Una specie di rito selvaggio dove la religione é rappresentata dal massimo sforzo: un viaggio lungo, faticoso e pieno di mille insidie che dura appena due giorni e una notte. Per due giorni questi atleti vivono insieme nello stadio, formano una comunita' attenta sola ai loro problemi, partecipano alle loro emozioni e aspettano il momento in cui uno di loro sara' proclamato il «miglior atleta del mondo». Purtroppo in base al miglior punteggio conseguito. Restano insieme dimostrando una grande fraternita' in attesa del loro turno di sofferenza come dei frati trappisti. Il pubblico sembra seguirli distrattamente nel loro calvario fino alla sera del secondo giorno quando manca l'ultima fatica: quella dei terribili 1500 metri. Ed é proprio qui che gli spettatori – così come quelli dei circhi romani osannavano il gladiatore vittorioso – come in un rito magico si levano in piedi, gridano e acclamano nella sua ultima fatica l'Ercole moderno. E gli Dei viventi di Montreal sono stati l'americano Jenner e le tedesche orientali Siegl e Laser. Le tedesche hanno totalizzato il medesimo punteggio di 4725.

GRAN PRIX

All'indomani, sempre allo «Stade Olimpique» i caroselli del Gran Premio per Nazioni di equitazione introducono i temi dell'addio. S'impone la Francia (che ottiene la seconda medaglia d'oro) davanti ai cavalieri della Germania Federale e del Belgio. L'Italia, quasi sempre vittoriosa nelle competizioni equestri, ne esce con le ossa rotte dei colonnelli d'Inzeo, assurri sin dalle Olimpiadi di Londra del '48.

Si attendono pero' le celebrazioni di una fine che si vorrebbe rimandare o per lo meno ritardare. Nella penombra dello stadio entrano le tribu' indiane guidate dai loro capi e gli esquimesi. Scortano gli atleti al centro del campo ed essi – i primi abitanti e proprietari di queste terre – danno in benvenuto ai Giochi proprio nel giorno della chiusura. Non é un addio. Lo sport ha vinto la sua battaglia anche se, come al termine di un grande spettacolo, il tabellone indica la fine. Sul tripode la fiamma é spenta. L'ultima notte dell'Olimpiade dell'arte e della cultura richiama tutti i protagonisti nel simbolico abbraccio finale. Montreal passa a Mosca il testimone di una staffetta che si corre da molti lustri e che, si spera, possa resistere a tutte le tentazioni che con lo sport non hanno niente da spartire. Non ultimo il gesto avventato di un nudista, un certo Michel Leduc, in cerca di pubblicita' su un palcosenico che non puo' assegnargli un ruolo.

Dans le stade, les équipes se rassemblent
pour la cérémonie d'ouverture tandis
que les danseurs apportent couleur et
éclat à la scène des futures compétitions.

Inside the stadium, the teams gather
for the opening ceremonies as dancers
add even more color and gaiety to the
scene of the impending competitions.

Im Stadion versammeln sich die Teams
für die Eröffnungsfeier. Volkstanzgruppen
tragen zur Buntheit der Szene bei.

Nello stadio, le squadre si radunano per
la cerimonia di apertura mentre i danzatori
contribuiscono con colori e gioia all'
attesa per le imminenti competizioni.

Le premier jour des compétitions voit des pelotons cyclistes commencer la course.

The first day of competition sees an assembly of cyclists start the race.

Am ersten Wettkampftag beginnen die Radfahrer ihr Rennen.

Ciclisti riuniti per dar inizio alla gara nel primo giorno dei giochi.

Le Canada a gagné une médaille de bronze dans le relais 4 x 100 mètres 4 nages, avec Wendy Hogg (dos), Robin Corsiglia (brasse), Susan Sloan (papillon) et Anne Jardin, que l'on voit ci-dessous dans la partie nage libre de l'épreuve. Wendy Hogg de Vancouver fait partie de l'équipe nationale depuis 1971; Robin Corsiglia, Beaconsfield, Québec, fut, à 13 ans, le plus jeune membre de l'équipe; Susan Sloan de Stettler, Alberta, participe aux championnats nationaux depuis 1974; Anne Jardin de Pointe-Claire, Québec, fait aussi partie de l'équipe nationale de natation depuis 1974. A côté des canadiennes se trouvent deux membres de l'équipe de la RDA médaillée d'or, dont le temps, de 4:07.95, est un nouveau record mondial et olympique. L'équipe canadienne a fait un temps de 4:15.22, à deux tiers de secondes seulement des médaillées d'argent.

Canada won a bronze medal in the women's 4 x 100 meter medley relay with the team of Wendy Hogg (backstroke), Robin Corsiglia (breaststroke), Susan Sloan (butterfly) and Anne Jardin, who is shown below as she swims the freestyle portion of the race. Wendy Hogg of Vancouver has been a member of the National Swim Team since 1971; from Beaconsfield, Quebec, Robin Corsiglia was the youngest member of the team at 13; Susan Sloan of Stettler, Alberta, has competed in the National Championships since 1974; Anne Jardin of Pointe-Claire, Quebec, has also been a National Swim Team member since 1974. Beside the Canadian performers stand two members of the gold medal-winning team from the GDR. Their winning time was 4:07.95, for a new world and Olympic record. The Canadian team had a time of 4:15.22, only two-thirds of a second away from the silver medallists.

Kanada gewann eine Bronzemedaille in der 4 x 100m Lagenstaffel der Frauen mit dem Team Wendy Hogg (Rücken), Robin Corsiglia (Brust), Susan Sloan (Delphin) und Anne Jardin unten, während des Wettkampfes. Wendy Hogg, Vancouver, gehört seit 1971 dem Nationalen Schwimmteam an: die dreizehn jährige Robin Corsiglia aus Beaconsfield, Quebec, war das jüngste Mitglied der Staffel; Susan Sloan aus Stettler, Alberta, hat seit 1974 an den Nationalmeisterschaften teilgenommen; Anne Jardin aus Pointe Claire, Quebec, ist gleichfalls seit 1974 Mitglied der Nationalmannschaft. Neben den kanadischen Schwimmerinnen stehen zwei Mitglieder der Siegerstaffel der DDR. Sie gewann die Goldene mit dem neuen Weltrekord von 4:07.95. Die Kanadierinnen schwammen 4:15.22 und blieben damit nur zwei Drittel einer Sekunde hinter den Silbermedaillenträgerinnen zurück.

Il Canada vince la medaglia di bronzo nella staffetta 4 x 100m femminile 4 stili con la squadra formata da Wendy Hogg (dorso), Robin Corsiglia (rana), Susan Sloan (farfalla), e Anne Jardin, mostrata sotto, mentre nuota la frazione stile libero della gara. Wendy Hogg di Vancouver é stata componente della squadra nazionale di nuoto sin dal 1971; Robin Corsiglia, 13 anni, di Beaconsfield, Quebec, é la più giovane della squadra; Susan Sloan di Stettler, Alberta, ha partecipato ai campionati nazionali sin dal 1974; Anne Jardin di Pointe-Claire, Quebec, ha fatto parte anche lei, della squadra nazionale di nuoto sin dal 1974. Accanto alle canadesi vediamo 2 componenti della squadra della Germania est, vincitrici della medaglia d'oro. Il loro tempo: 4:07,95, nuovo record mondiale ed olimpico. La squadra canadese 4:15,22 due terzi di secondo appena dalle vincitrici della medaglia d'argento.

Bryan Gibson, Canada.

Iuliaka Semenova, URSS/USSR.

Les japonaises battent les canadiennes 121:89. A droite, les É-U battent le Canada 95-77 lors de la demi-finale hommes.

The Japanese women defeat Canada 121:89. Right, the USA defeats Canada 95:77 in the men's semi-finals.

Die Japanerinnen schlagen Canada 121:89. Rechts: die USA siegt über Kanada 95:77 in der Vorschlussrunde der Männer.

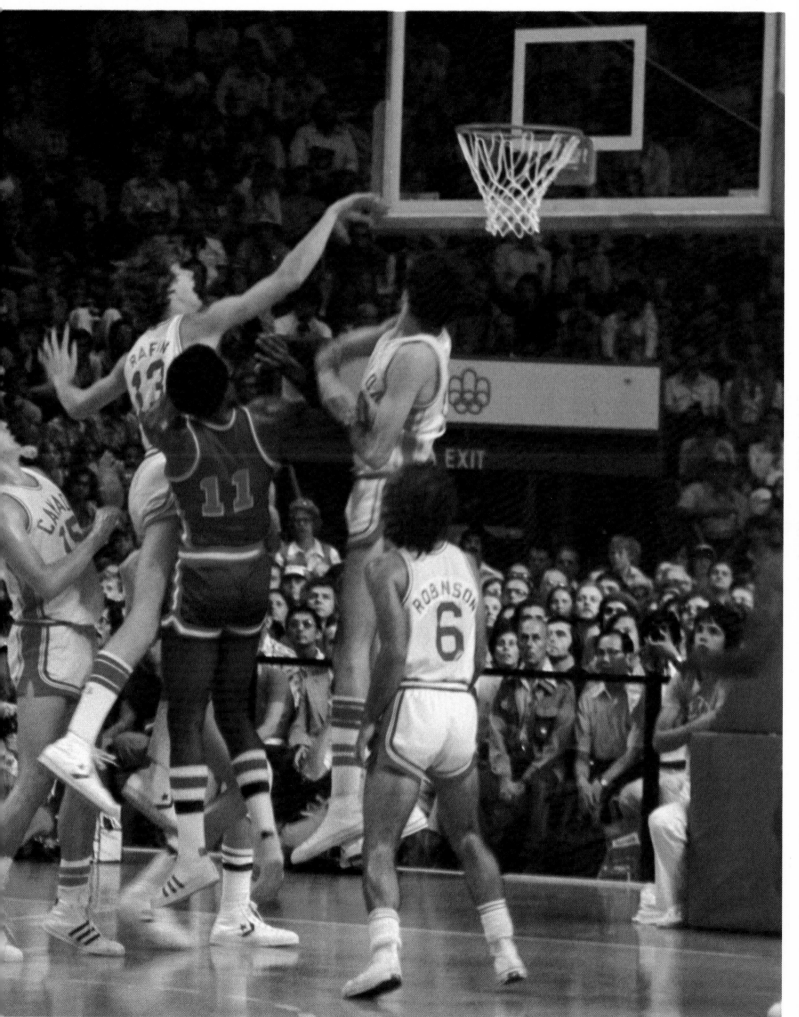

Le ragazze giapponice battono il Canada 98:75. Destra, gli USA battono il Canada 95:77 nelle semifinali maschili.

John Naber, É-U, une médaille d'argent et quatre d'or. Naber a gagné le 100 mètres dos en 55.49 et le 200 mètres dos en 1:59.19, nouveaux records du monde. Il fit partie de l'équipe victorieuse du 4 x 200 mètres, qui a établi un record du monde de 7:23.22, et de celle du 4 x 100 mètres 4 nages, qui gagna en établissant un nouveau record de 3:49.22.

John Naber of the USA, who won a silver medal and four golds. Naber won the 100 meter backstroke in 55.49 seconds and the 200 meter backstroke in 1:59.19, both new world records. He was a member of the victorious team in the 4 x 200m freestyle, which set a world record of 7:23.22, and of the 4 x 100m medley, which won with a new record of 3:49.22.

John Naber, USA, der eine Silberne und vier Goldene mit heimnahm. Naber gewann das 100m Rückenschwimmen in 55.49 Sekunden und die 200m Rücken in 1:59.19; beide Zeiten sind neue Weltbestleistungen. Er war ein Mitglied der siegreichen 4 x 200m Freistilstaffel, die einen Weltrekord von 7:23.22 aufstellte, und der 4 x 100m Lagenstaffel, die mit der neuen Bestleistung von 3:49.22 siegte.

L'americano John Naber che ha vinto una medaglia d'argento e 4 d'oro. Naber ha vinto i 100m dorso in 55.49 secondi e i 200m dorso in 1:59.19, ambedue nuovi record mondiali. Ha fatto parte della squadra vincitrice della 4 x 200m stile libero, che ha stabilito il primato mondiale in 7:23.22, come pure della 4 x 100m mista, che ha vinto stabilendo un nuovo record di 3:49.22.

Sur le plan d'eau de Kingston, Ontario, les concurrents de toutes classes profitèrent du beau temps et du bon vent lors de leur course aux médailles.

At the Kingston, Ontario, sailing site, sailors in boats of all classes enjoyed fair weather and fine winds as they vied for position and possible medals.

In Kingston, Ontario, dem Schauplatz der Segelwettbewerbe, hatten die Segler günstigen Wind, als sie miteinander um ihre Positionen und um den Sieg segelten.

A Kingston, Ontario, dove si svolgono le gare veliche, i partecipanti, su barche di varie classi, sono stati favoriti dal bel tempo e da un buon vento, nelle gare per la classifica e le medaglie.

*Les voiles ondulent
tandis que
la flamme olympique
monte la garde.*

*Sails billow
as the Kingston
Olympic flame
stands guard.*

*Segel blähen sich,
und die Olympische
Flamme von Kingston
steht Wacht.*

*Le vele si
gonfiano mentre
la fiamma olimpica
domina la scena.*

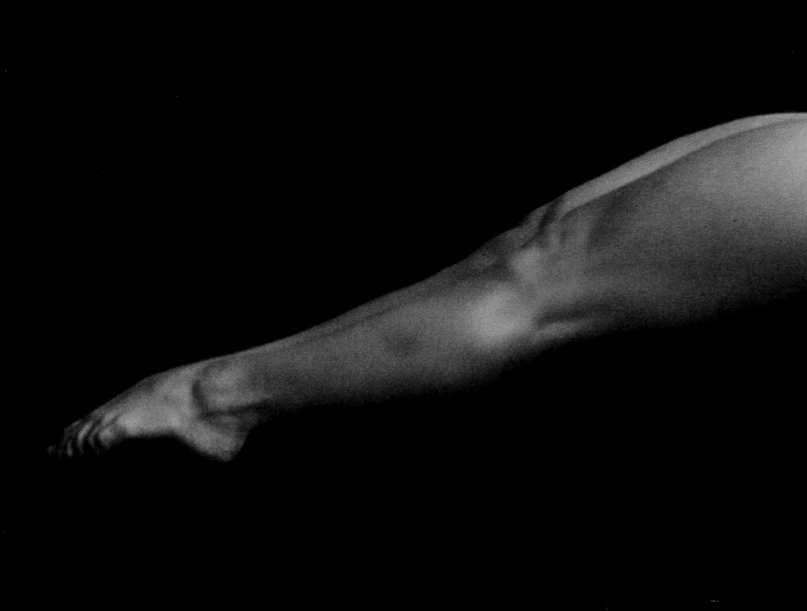

Dans le superbe vélodrome des cyclistes aux muscles bandés tournent sur la piste au virage rélevé, associant adresse, stratégie et vitesse en quête d'une médaille d'or.

In the spectacular new Velodrome tense-muscled cyclists whirl around the banked track as they combine skill, strategy and speed in the search for gold.

Im imposanten neuen Velodrom flitzen Radfahrer, alle Muskeln angespannt, um die Bahn; Geschicklichkeit, Geschwindigkeit und Strategie können ihnen bei der Goldsuche zum Erfolg verhelfen.

Nel nuovo spettacolare velodromo, i ciclisti con i muscoli tesi, corrono intorno alla pista dando prova di strategia e velocità nella loro caccia all'oro.

Nelli Kim, URSS, une des préférées de la foule, gagna des médailles d'or au saut de cheval (avec une note parfaite) et aux exercices au sol. A ceci, elle ajouta une médaille d'argent lors des épreuves individuelles.

Nelli Kim of the USSR, one of the crowd's favorites. She won golds in the vault (with a perfect score) and in the floor exercises. To these she added a silver medal for best all around.

Nelli Kim, UdSSR gehörte zu den Publikumslieblingen. Sie gewann Gold im Gerätespringen (mit der Note 10) und im Bodenturnen, und Silber mit der Mannschaft.

La russa Nelli Kim, una delle favorite del pubblico, ha vinto le medaglie d'oro nel volteggio (con punteggio perfetto) e negli esercizi a corpo libero. Ha inoltre vinto la medaglia d'argento nella classifica generale.

Nancy McDonnell, Canada.

Olga Korbut, URSS, héroine
des Jeux de 1972, et bien
qu'elle reste encore une
favorite, a vu son étoile
éclipsée par celle d'une
nouvelle athlète plus jeune.
Elle a aidé son équipe a
remporter une médaille d'or
et a elle-même gagné une
médaille d'argent.

Olga Korbut of the USSR,
heroine of the 1972 Games,
now outshone by a newer,
younger star, though still a
favorite with the crowd.
She helped bring her team
a gold and won an individual
silver medal.

Olga Korbutt, UdSSR,
gefeierte Siegerin der Spiele
in München wurde, obwohl
immer noch Favoritin des
Publikums, durch einen neuen,
jüngeren Stern überschattet.
Sie verhalf jedoch ihrer
Mannschaft zu Gold und bekam
selbst Silber.

La russa Olga Korbut, eroina
dei giochi del '72,
detronizzata dalla nuova
e più giovane vedetta,
ma sempre favorita del
pubblico. Aiutò la sua
squadra a vincere una
medaglia d'oro e vinse per
se una medaglia d'argento.

Epreuves d'escrime.
Ci-dessous, Ecaterina Stahl
(64), Roumanie, rencontre
Margarita Rodriguez (16), Cuba.

The fencers at work.
Below, Ecaterina Stahl (64) of
Rumania meets Margarita
Rodriguez (16) of Cuba.

Die Fechter kreuzen die Klingen.
Unten: Ecaterina Stahl (64),
Rumänien, gegen Margarita
Rodriguez (16), Cuba.

Gli schermitori in azione.
Sotto, la rumena Ecaterina Stahl (64)
incontra la cubana Margarita Rodriguez

L'engagement physique total n'a peut-être jamais été aussi apparent que lors des épreuves de lutte.

Perhaps nowhere else than in the wrestling did the completeness of the struggle between athletes show more fully or more openly.

In kaum einer Disziplin zeigt sich der Kampf der beiden Gegner klarer und deutlicher als im Ringkampf.

Nessun' altra gara come la lotta libera mostra con tale completezza lo sforzo della lotta tra gli atleti.

Nadia Comaneci. La jeune roumaine obtint les notes parfaites de 10 sept fois durant la compétition. Elle gagna 3 médailles d'or, 1 d'argent et 1 de bronze au grand ravissement des spectateurs. Avec quelle grâce et quel sens de la précision effectua-t-elle ses exercices! Par moment tout semblait rendu simple par cette toute petite fille: mais, comme l'indique la photo de gauche, tout cela n'était pas aussi simple et aisé. La fatigue, le dévouement constant et de longues heures de travail dur et répétitif font des champions comme Nadia Comaneci.

The great Nadia Comaneci of Rumania, who was given perfect scores of 10 seven times during the competition. She won 3 golds, 1 silver and 1 bronze to the delight of the audience. How gracefully and with what a sense of timing and beauty she carried out her routines! At times it all seemed to be made simple by this tiny girl: but, as the picture on the left shows, it was not all ease and fluidity. Tension and dedication and endless hours of hard, repetitive work make champions like Nadia Comaneci.

Nadia Comaneci aus Rumänien. Sie begeisterte die Zuschauer mit ihren perfekten Übungen. Siebenmal wurde ihr die perfekte Punktzahl 10 verliehen und sie holte sich 3 x Gold, 1 x Silber und 1 x Bronze. Mit Beschwingtheit, Tempo und Anmut führte sie ihre Übungen aus! Wie das Bild links zeigt, war es nicht nur Spiel, sondern auch Anspannung und Konzentration.

Nadia Comaneci. Alla giovane rumena fu assegnato il punteggio pieno di 10 sette volte durante le gare. Ed essa vinse 3 medaglie d'oro, 1 d'argento ed 1 di bronze tra il delirio della folla. Con quale grazia, tempismo e bellezza essa svolse i suoi esercizi! E lei così gracile riusciva a far sembrar tutto così facile: ma, come mostra la fotografia a sinistra non era tutto così facile e fluido. La tensione, la dedizione ed infinite ore di duro lavoro formano i campioni come Nadia Comaneci.

John Naber applaudit les équipiers de l'équipe canadienne du relais 4 x 100m nage tandis qu'ils reçoivent leurs médailles d'argent. Ce sont Stephen Pickell de Vancouver, Graham Smith d'Edmonton, Clay Evans, qui s'entraîne à Huntingdon Beach, Californie, et Gary MacDonald de Mission, C.B. Dans la piscine, Graham Smith.

John Naber applauds as the members of the Canadian 4 x 100m medley relay team accept their silver medals. They are Stephen Pickell of West Vancouver, Graham Smith of Edmonton, Clay Evans, who swims out of Huntingdon Beach, California, and Gary MacDonald of Mission, B.C. The man in the pool is Graham Smith.

Das Team der kanadischen 4 x 100m Lagenstaffel erhält ihre Silbermedaille und John Naber applaudiert ihnen. Die Kanadier sind Stephen Pickell aus West Vancouver, Graham Smith aus Edmonton, Clay Evans, der in Huntingdon Beach, Kalifornien, trainiert und Gary MacDonald aus Mission, Britisch Kolumbien. Der Mann im Bassin ist Graham Smith.

Mentre John Naber, membro della squadra americana vincitrice della medaglia d'oro applaude, i componenti della squadra canadese della staffetta 4 x 100m mista ricevono le medaglie d'argento. Essi sono Stephen Pickell di Vancouver ovest, Graham Smith di Edmonton, Clay Evans, di Huntingdon Beach, California e Gary MacDonald di Mission, B.C. L'atleta in piscina é Graham Smith.

Alexander Oakley, 48 ans, participant au 20 kilomètres marche, était le plus âgé de l'équipe canadienne. Ce furent ses cinquièmes Olympiades.

Alexander Oakley, an entrant in the 20 kilometer walk, was the oldest member of the Canadian team, at 48. These were his fifth Olympics.

Alexander Oakley, ein Teilnehmer im 20 km-Gehen, war mit seinen 48 Jahren das älteste Mitglied der kanadischen Mannschaft. Das war seine fünfte Olympiade.

Alexander Oakley, iscritto alla 20 km di marcia era il più anziano della squadra canadese a 48 anni. Queste erano le sue quinte Olimpiadi.

Concurrentes montrant
l'élan, le saut et
la réception du saut
en longueur.

Women competitors
show an approach, the
leap, and a landing
in the long jump.

Leichtathletinnen im
Anlauf, beim Sprung
und der Landung
im Weitsprung.

Partecipanti femminili
nel salto in lungo
mostrano la rincorsa, il
salto e l'atterraggio.

A gauche, Nikolai Andrianov, URSS, en action.
Ci-dessous à droite, le canadien Pierre Leclerc de Sainte-Thérèse, Québec.

At left, Nikolai Andrianov of the USSR goes through a routine.
Below right, Canadian Pierre Leclerc of Sainte-Therese, Quebec.

Links: Nikolai Andrianov, UdSSR, während seiner Übung.
Unten rechts: Der Kanadier Pierre Leclerc aus Sainte-Therese, Quebec.

A sinistra il russo Nikolai Andrianov esegue un esercizio.
Sotto a destra il canadese Pierre Leclerc di Ste-Therese, Quebec.

*Hasely Crawford (846), Trinité, reste
un court instant à la hauteur des
autres athlètes, avant de jaillir
et gagner la médaille d'or du 100 mètres.*

Ruth Fuchs, RDA, se prépare
à lancer le javelot lors de
l'épreuve qu'elle gagna avec
un jet de 65,94 mètres,
nouveau record Olympique.

Ruth Fuchs of the GDR prepares
to throw the javelin in an
event she won with a toss of
65.94 meters, a new record.

Ruth Fuchs, DDR, nimmt Anlauf
für den Speerwurf. Sie siegte
in dieser Disziplin mit einem
Wurf von 65,94m und stellte
gleichzeitig einen neuen
Olympischen-Rekord auf.

La tedesca orientale Ruth
Fuchs si prepara a lanciare
il giavellotto nella gara
che ha vinto con un lancio di
65,94m, nuovo record olimpico.

*Karen Smith, É-U, qui
termina huitième, avec un
jet de 57,50 mètres.*

*Karen Smith, USA, die
mit 57,50m Achte wurde.*

*Karen Smith of the USA, who
finished eighth, throwing
for 57.50 meters.*

*L'americana Karen Smith 8a
con un lancio di 57,50m.*

Bruce Jenner, É-U/USA.

Concurrents au lancer du poids.
En bas à droite, Evgeni Nironov,
URSS, argent; Udo Beyer, RDA, or;
Barisnikov, bronze. Barisnikov,
lors des épreuves éliminatoires,
avait établi un nouveau record
Olympique avec 21,32 mètres,
mais il ne termina que troisième
lors de la finale.

Competitors in the shot put.
Bottom right, Evgeni Nironov,
USSR, silver; Udo Beyer, GDR,
gold; Barisnikov, bronze.
Barisnikov had set a new Olympic
record of 21.32 meters in the
qualifying round, but could only
finish third in the final round.

Teilnehmer am Kugelstosswett-
bewerb. Unten rechts: Evgeni
Nironov, UdSSR, Silber; Udo
Beyer, DDR, Gold, Barisnikov,
Bronze. Barisnikov, der in der
Ausscheidungsrunde einen neuen
Olympischen-Rekord von 21,32m
aufgestellt hatte, musste sich im
Endkampf mit dem dritten
Platz begnügen.

Atleti nella gara del peso.
Sotto a destra, il russo Evgeni
Nironov, medaglia d'argento;
il tedesco dell'est Udo Beyer,
medaglia d'oro; Barisnikov,
bronzo. Barisnikov ha stabilito un
nuovo record olimpico di 21,32m
nei lanci de qualificazione,
ma si qualificava solo terzo
nei lanci per la finale.

Trois équipes canadiennes d'aviron, les deux et quatre sans barreur, et le huit barré.

Three Canadian rowing teams, the coxless pairs and fours, and the coxed eights.

Drei kanadische Rudermannschaften, der Zweier und Vierer ohne Steuermann und der Achter mit Steuermann.

Tre equipaggi canadesi di canottaggio, il doppio e il quattro senza timoniere, e l'otto con timoniere.

*La Princesse Anne,
participante la plus
célèbre de ces jeux.*

*Princess Anne,
the most prominent
entrant in these
Olympic games.*

*Prinzessin Anne,
die prominenteste
Teilnehmerin an
diesen Spielen.*

*La Principessa Anne,
la partecipante più
famosa in questi
giochi.*

dernier en date des héros
landais, Lasse Viren, en
in triomphe. Il a remporté
ıx médailles d'or pour le
Om et le 10 000m. Essayant
n obtenir une troisième au
rathon, il a terminé 5ème.

The latest hero from Finland,
Lasse Viren, in the pack and
in triumph. He won gold medals
in the 5000m and 10 000m.
Trying for the triple win, he
entered in the marathon, and
finished a respectable fifth.

Lasse Viren, Finnlands neu
entdeckter Held, triumphierend
inmitten der Wettbewerber.
Er gewann Gold im 5000m und
10 000m Lauf. Der dreifache Sieg
blieb ihm versagt, im Marathon-
Lauf belegte Lasse Viren «nur»
den fünften Platz.

L'ultimo eroe finlandese,
Lasse Viren, mentre é nel gruppo
e nel momento del trionfo.
Ha vinto le medaglie d'oro
nei 5000 e 10 000m. Tentando di
vincere una tripletta, ha
partecipato alla maratona,
finendo però 5o.

Tatiana Kazankina, URSS,
a gagné une médaille d'or
au 800m, établissant de
nouveaux records olympiques
et mondiaux avec 1:54.94.
Elle a obtenu une deuxième
médaille d'or au 1500m.

Tatiana Kazankina of the
USSR team won a gold medal
in the 800m, setting a new
Olympic and world record
of 1:54.94. She added a
second gold medal by
winning in the 1500m.

Zweimal erlief sich Tatiana
Kazankina, UdSSR, Gold.
Mit einem neuen Olympia-
und Weltrekord, in der Zeit
von 1:54.94 im 800m Lauf
und in der 1500m Strecke.

Tatiana Kazankina della
squadra russa ha vinto la
medaglia d'oro negli 800m,
stabilendo il nuovo record
olimpico e mondiale di
1:54.94. Ha ottenuto una
seconda medaglia vincendo
i 1500m.

Rosemarie Ackermann, GDR,
a gagné une médaille
d'or au saut en hauteur,
établissant un nouveau
record olympique avec 1,93m.

In the women's high jump,
Rosemarie Ackermann, GDR,
below, won a gold medal and
set a new Olympic record
with a jump of 1.93m.

Im Hochsprung der Frauen
stellte Rosemarie Ackermann,
DDR, einen neuen Olympia-
rekord von 1,93m auf und
gewann die Goldmedaille.

Nel salto in alto femminile.
Rosemarie Ackermann
della Germania est (sotto)
ha vinto la medaglia
d'oro e stabilito il nuovo
record olimpico con 1,93m.

La Canadienne
Debbie Brill n'a
malheureusement
pu se qualifier.

Debbie Brill aus
Kanada konnte sich
nicht qualifizieren.

Unfortunately,
Canada's Debbie
Brill, using the
famous flop style,
failed to qualify.

Sfortunatamente
la canadese
Debbie Brill
non riusciva
a qualificarsi.

Le saut à la perche fut remporté par le
Polonais Tadeusz Slusarski, qui a
égalé le record olympique de 5,50m. Les
concurrents arrivés 2ème et 3ème ont
égalé ce record, mais le classement s'est
fait en fonction du nombre d'essais.
Wladysla Kozakiewicz s'est qualifié
mais a terminé 11ème.

The pole vault was a closely-contested
event, won by Tadeusz Slusarski of Poland,
equalling the Olympic record of 5.50m.
The second and third place finishers also
equalled that record, and positions were
determined on the basis of the number of
attempts made. His teammate, Wladysla
Kozakiewicz, qualified easily but slipped
to eleventh place in the final.

Im Stabhochsprung siegte Tadeusz Slusarski,
Polen. Mit 5,50m stellte er den neuen
Olympiarekord ein. Die Wettkämpfer, die
den zweiten und dritten Platz belegten,
erzielten zwar die gleiche Höhe, die
Klassifizierung erfolgte jedoch anhand
der Anzahl ihrer Versuche. Mannschafts-
kollege Wladysla Kozakiewicz qualifizierte
sich ohne Mühe, fiel aber im Finale auf
den elften Platz zurück.

Il salto con l'asta fu una gara molto
combattuta vinta dal polacco Tadeusz
Slusarski che eguagliava il primato del
mondo di 5,50m. Il record veniva egua-
gliato dal 2º e 3º classificato e la
classifica finale veniva stabilita in
base al numero dei tentativi. Il suo
compagno di squadra, Wladysla Kozakiewicz,
si qualificava facilmente, ma in finale
non andava al di là dell'11º posto.

Phil Olsen, CAN.

Seppo Hovinen, FIN.

est le célèbre Vasili Alexeev qui remporté la médaille d'or de catégorie poids super-lourd.

In the super heavyweight class, snatch and clean and jerk, the popular Vasili Alexeev won the gold medal.

Der populäre Gewichtheber, Vasili Alexeev, UdSSR, Goldmedaillengewinner im Super-Schwergewicht.

Nella categoria dei super massimi del sollevamento pesi, il popolare Vasili Alexeev vince la medaglia d'oro.

En haut à gauche, la Canadienne Susan Stewart (13) contre la Polonaise Kamilla Skladanowska au fleuret. En bas, à gauche, la Canadienne Chantal Payer (12) rencontre la Polonaise Krystyna Machnicka-Urbans. L'équipe Canadienne a été éliminée. A droite, Susan Stewart regarde pensivement son fleuret à côté de Donna Hennyey.

Top left, Canada's Susan Stewart (13) against Poland's Kamilla Skladanowska in the ladies' foil team event. Below left, Canada's Chantal Payer (12) meets fencer Krystyna Machnicka-Urbans of Poland. The Canadian team was eliminated. At right, Susan Stewart pensively examines her foil while towel-draped teammate Donna Hennyey looks on.

Oben links, Kanadas Susan Stewart (13) gegen Kamilla Skladanowska, Polen, im Florett-fechten. Unten links, Kanadas Chantal Payer (12) im Duell mit Krystyna Machnicka-Urbans aus Polen. Kanadas Mannschaft konnte sich nicht qualifizieren. Rechts, Susan Stewart betrachtet gedankenvoll ihr Florett, während Mannschaftskol-legin Donna Hennyey zuschaut.

La canadese Susan Stewart, in alto a sinistra (13) contro la polacca Kamilla Skladanowska nella gara di fioretto a squadre femminile. La canadese Chantal Payer (12), sotto sinistra, incontra la schermitrice polacca Krystyna Machnicka-Urbans. La squadra canadese veniva eliminata. Susan Stewart, a destra, guarda pensosa il suo fioretto mentre la compagna di squadra Donna Hennyey, avvolta da un asciugamano, osserva.

Michel Vaillancourt a été le premier Canadien à remporter une médaille au saut Grand Prix.

Michel Vaillancourt was the first Canadian to win a medal in the individual Grand Prix show jumping.

Michel Vaillancourt, der erste Kanadier, der im Grand Prix Einzelspringen eine Medaille gewann.

Michel Vaillancourt, il primo canadese a vincere una medaglia nel Grand Prix del salto individuale.

De gauche à droite, Michel Vaillancourt, médaille d'argent; François Mathy, Belgique, médaille de bronze et Alwin Schockemöhle, Allemagne de l'Ouest, médaille d'or.

Left to right, Michel Vaillancourt, silver medal; François Mathy of Belgium bronze medal; and Alwin Schockemöhle of West Germany, the gold medal winner.

Von links nach rechts Michel Vaillancourt, Silber; Belgiens François Mathy, Bronze und Alwin Schockemöhle, BRD, Gold.

Da sinistra a destra, Michel Vaillancourt, medaglia d'argento; il belga François Mathy medaglia di bronzo; ed il tedesco occidentale Alwin Schockemöhle, vincitore della medaglia d'oro.

Klaus Dibiasi, Italie, a remporté la médaille d'or au plongeon. Il est le premier à obtenir des médailles d'or dans trois Olympiades, Munich en 1972, Mexico en 1968 et Montréal.

Klaus Dibiasi of Italy won the gold medal in platform diving. He is the first man to have won gold medals in three separate Olympics in this event, accomplishing the feat both at Munich in 1972 and Mexico City in 1968.

Klaus Dibiasi, Italien, gewann die Goldmedaille im Turmspringen. Der erste Turmspringer, der auf drei Olympiaden eine Goldmedaille in dieser Disziplin gewann: Mexico City, München, Montreal.

L'italiano Klaus Dibiasi vincitore della medaglia d'oro nella gara di tuffi dalla piattaforma. Egli é il primo uomo ad aver vinto la medaglia d'oro in questa gara in 3 diverse Olimpiadi e cioé a Monaco nel '72 ed a Messico City nel '68.

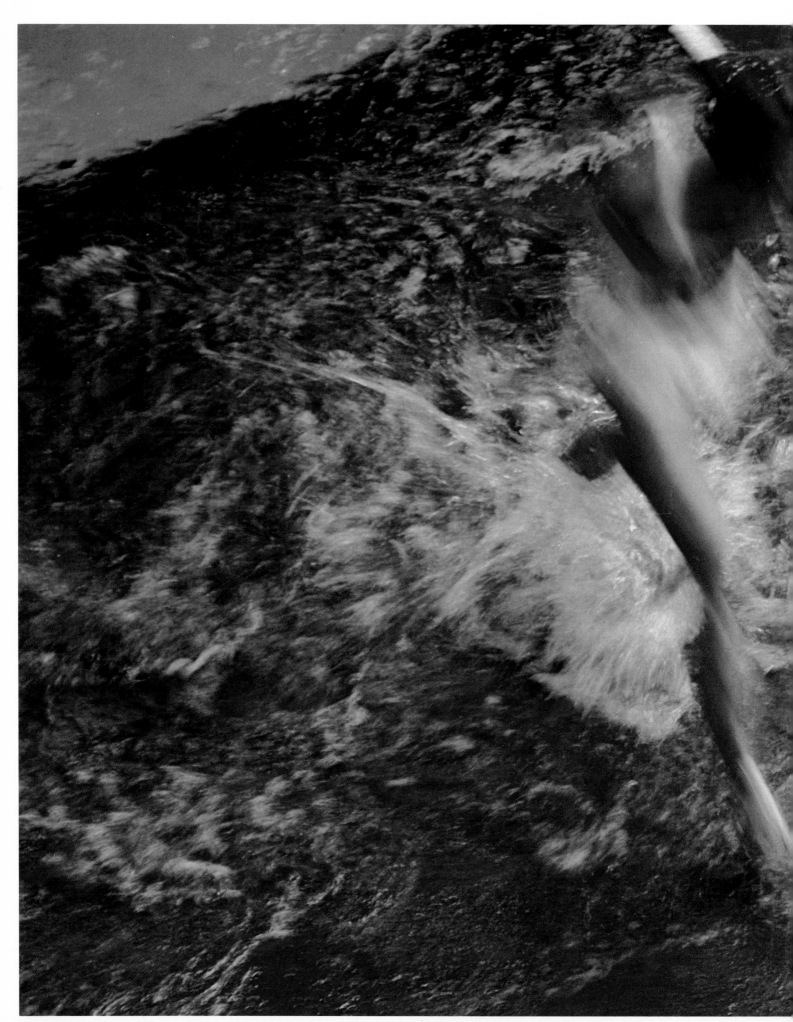

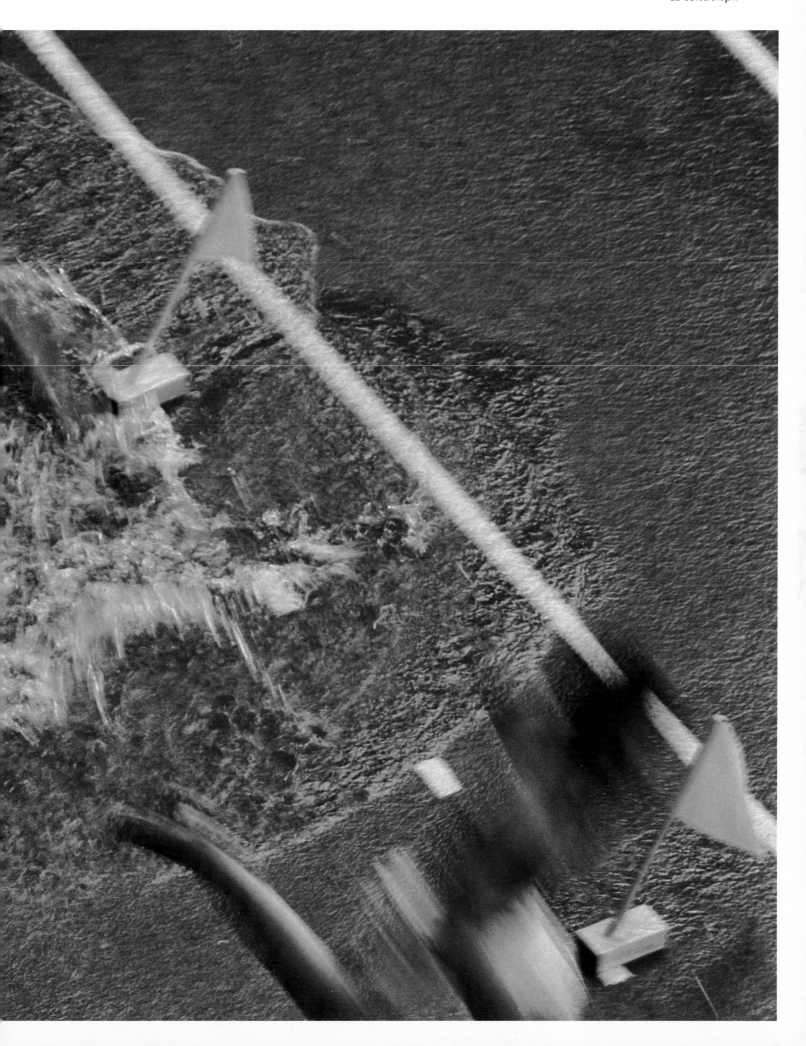

Alejandro Casanas, Cuba, a remporté la médaille d'argent au 110m haies terminant en 13.33. Guy Drut, France, a remporté la médaille d'or avec 13.30.

Alejandro Casanas of Cuba took the silver medal in the 110m hurdles, lowering his time with each successive heat. His final time was 13.33, but Guy Drut of France won the gold medal with a time of 13.30.

Kubas Alejandro Casanas sicherte sich die Silbermedaille im 110m Hürdenlauf, indem er seine Zwischenzeiten ständig verbesserte. Seine Zeit betrug 13.33 Sek. Die Goldene ging an Guy Drut, Frankreich, mit einer Zeit von 13.30 Sekunden.

Il cubano Alejandro Casanas, che ha
vinto la medaglia d'argento nei 110m ad
ostacoli, abbassando il suo tempo in ogni
batteria. Il suo tempo nella finale fu di
13.33, ma il francese Guy Drut vinse
la medaglia d'oro con il tempo di 13.30.

Le Canadien Grant McLaaren juste avant
l'incident controversé dans la course
5000m. Willy Polleunis et Klaus
Hildenbrand l'ont encerclé à 200m de
la fin. Ian Stewart, Grande-Bretagne,
a pris le parti de McLaaren qui a fait
appel. L'appel a été pris en consi-
dération et McLaaren est passé de la
6ème à la 4ème place, dernier rang des
qualifications. Le Belge et l'Allemand
de l'Ouest ont été disqualifiés.
Mais le jury renversait sa décision,
redonnant leur place à Polleunis et
à Hildenbrand. McLaaren, 6ème, n'a
pu se qualifier pour la finale.

Grant McLaaren of Canada just prior
to the controversial jostling
incident in the qualifying heat of
the 5000m. This odd situation came
about when Willy Polleunis and Klaus
Hildenbrand sandwiched McLaaren with
200 meters left. Ian Stewart of
Great Britan claimed that McLaaren
had been fouled and an appeal was
launched. At first, the appeal was
allowed. McLaaren was advanced from
sixth to fourth place, the last
qualifying rank, and the Belgian
and West German runners were
disqualified. But the jury of appeal
reversed its decision that evening,
reinstating Polleunis and Hildenbrand. Grant McLaaren was back in
sixth place and out of the final.

Grant McLaaren, Kanada, kurz vor der
umstrittenen Behinderung im 5000m Lauf.
Diese Situation entstand dadurch, dass
McLaaren 200m vor dem Ziel von
Willy Polleunis und Klaus Hildenbrand
eingeklemmt wurde. Ian Stewart, England,
behauptete, McLaaren habe einen regel-
widrigen Stoss erhalten und es wurde
Berufung eingelegt. Zunächst wurde der
Beschwerde zugestimmt, McLaaren rückte
vom sechsten auf den vierten Platz,
wodurch er eine Runde weitergekommen
wäre. Der belgische und der westdeutsche
Läufer wurden disqualifiziert. Die
Jury machte jedoch am Abend ihre Ent-
scheidung wieder rückgängig. Grant
McLaaren rutschte somit wieder auf
den sechsten Platz und verlor seine
Chance für den Endlauf.

Il canadese Grant McLaaren, prima dell'
incidente che causava una controversia
nella batteria di qualificazione dei
5000m. Questa strana situazione si
verificò quando Willy Polleunis e Klaus
Hildenbrand schiacciarono tra loro
McLaaren a 200m dall'arrivo. L'inglese
Ian Stewart reclamò dicendo che McLaaren
era stato ostacolato e quindi fu
inoltrato un ricorso. All'inizio il
ricorso fu accolto e McLaaren fu riclas-
sificato dal 6° al 4° posto, ultimo per
la classificazione, e i corridori del
Belgio e della Germania occidentale
venivano squalificati. Ma la guiria
cambiò decisione la sera stessa riclas-
sificando Polleunis e Hildenbrand.
Grant McLaaren tornò quindi al 6° posto
fuori dalla finale.

Le bond qui rapporta
la médaille d'argent
à Randy Williams, É-U,
au saut en longueur.

Randy Williams, USA,
gibt sein Bestes,
dies brachte ihm
die Silberne im
Weitsprung.

Randy Williams, USA,
with his effort that
got him the silver
in the long jump.

Randy Williams, USA,
impegnato nello sforzo
che gli ha procurato
la medaglia d'argento
nel salto in lungo.

Au milieu, Tatiana Anisimova, URSS, qui gagna la médaille d'argent au 100m haies.

In the middle is Tatiana Anisimova of the USSR, who won the silver medal for the 100m hurdles.

In der Bildmitte: Tatiana Anisimova, UdSSR, die im 100m Hürdenlauf die Silberne errang.

Al centro la russa Tatiana Anisimova che ha vinto la medaglia d'argento nei 100m ostacoli.

Ci-dessus, Johanna Schaller, médaille d'or.

Above is the GDR's Johanna Schaller, gold.

Oben: Die Siegerin Johanna Schaller aus der DDR.

Sopra la tedesca dell'ést Johanna Schaller, medaglia d'oro.

*L'équipe d'URSS bat le Brésil
2:0 lors de la rencontre
pour la troisième place
du tournoi de football.*

*The USSR team beat Brazil 2:0
in the battle for third place
in the soccer tournament.*

*Die UdSSR schlug Brasilien
2:0 im Kampf um den dritten
Platz im Fussballturnier.*

*La squadra russa batte
il Brasile per 2:0 nella
lotta per il 3º posto
nel torneo di calcio.*

Médaille d'or du 400m,
Alberto Juantorena, Cuba,
jaugeant ses adversaires.

Gold medalist in the 400m, Alberto Juantorena of Cuba checking his opposition.

Goldmedaillengewinner im 400m Lauf, Alberto Juantorena, Kuba, schaut sich nach seinen Konkurrenten um.

La medaglia d'oro dei 400m, Alberto Juantorena di Cuba che si volta per controllare gli avversari.

Ci-dessous, John Wood de Toronto, s'envolant vers la médaille d'argent dans l'épreuve de canoë canadien sur une distance de 500m. A droite, une équipe de deux Suédois en plein effort.

Below, John Wood of Toronto, on his way to the silver medal in the Canadian canoe event over a 500m course. Right, a two-man team from Sweden at work.

Unten: John Wood aus Toronto, auf dem Weg zur Silbernen im Einer-Canadier über 500m. Rechts: Das schwedische Zweimann Boot im Wettbewerb.

Sotto, John Wood di Toronto si avvia verso la medaglia d'argento nella gara di canoa canadese su percorso di 500m. A destra, il doppio svedese in azione.

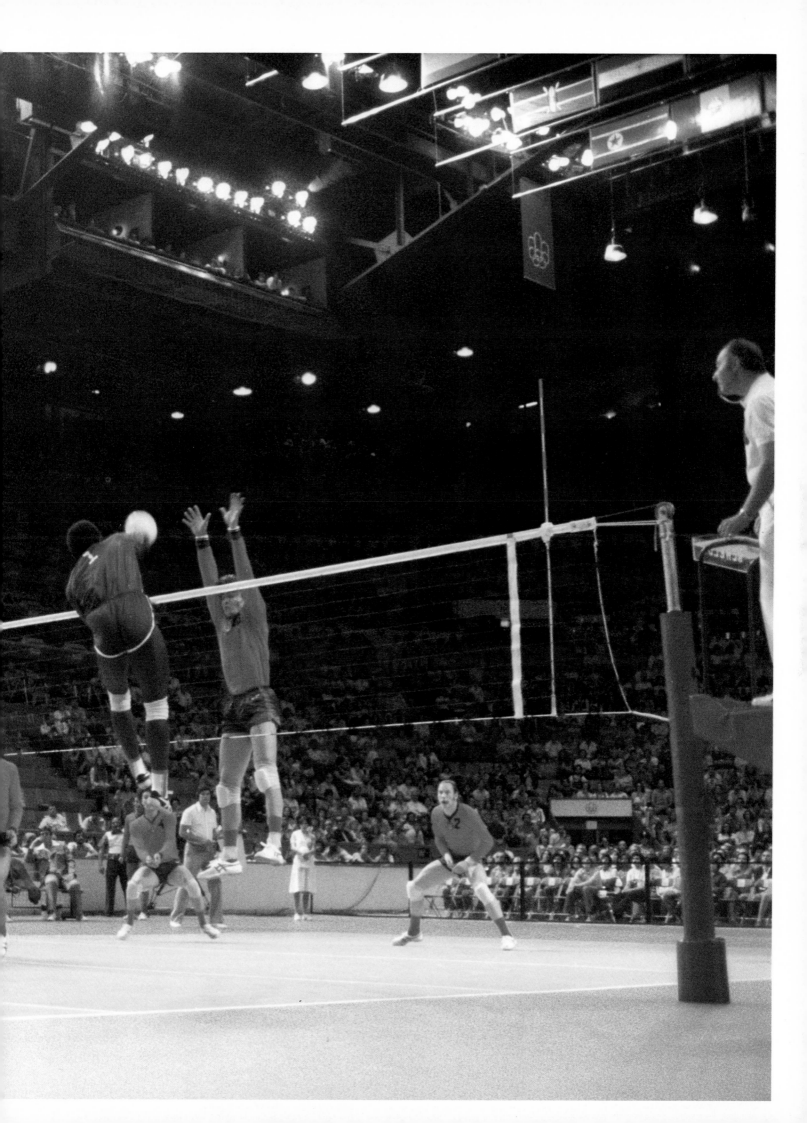

Sur la page précédente et à gauche, les Cubains battus par l'URSS 3:0 en demi-finale. A gauche, les Hongroises battirent les Canadiennes 3:1.

Previous page and left, the Cubans lost to the USSR, 3:0, in the semi-finals. At right, Hungary defeated the Canadian women three sets to one.

Vordere Seite und links: Die Kubaner verloren gegen das Team der UdSSR 3:0 im Halbfinale. Rechts: Die Ungarinnen schlugen die Kanadierinnen 3:1.

Nella pagina precedente ed a sinistra, i cubani perdenti per 3:0 contro la URSS nelle semi finali. A destra l'Ungheria che batte le ragazze canadesi per 4 partite ad uno.

Le roi des athlètes Bruce Jenner. Il gagna la médaille d'or établissant un nouveau record mondial du décathlon.
King of the Athletes, Bruce Jenner. He struck gold with a new world record in the decathlon.
Der König der Athleten, Bruce Jenner. Mit einem neuen Weltrekord holte er sich die Goldene im Zehnkampf.
Bruce Jenner, re degli atleti. Ghermisce la medaglia d'oro stabilendo il nuovo record del mondo nel decathlon.

Le Canadien Greg Joy de Vancouver. Il sauta 2,23m et gagna la médaille d'argent devant le favori Dwight Stones.

Canada's Greg Joy of Vancouver. He jumped 2.23m to win the silver medal ahead of controversial Dwight Stones.

Der Kanadier Greg Joy aus Vancouver. Er sprang 2,23m und gewann die Silberne vor dem favorisierten Dwight Stones.

Il canadese Greg Joy di Vancouver. Con un salto di 2,23m vinceva la medaglia d'argento precedendo il contestato Dwight Stones.

Les athlètes américains excellèrent dans
les courses de relais hommes. Ils ont
capturé l'or dans le 4 x 100m (ci-dessous)
et, le même jour, célébrèrent leur
victoire dans le 4 x 400m.

The U.S. athletes excelled in the men's relay races. They captured gold in the 4 x 100m (below) and on the same day celebrated their victory in the 4 x 400m.

Die Sportler aus den USA dominierten in den Staffelläufen. Sie erliefen Gold in der 4 x 100m (unten) und freuen sich über ihren Sieg am selben Tag in der 4 x 400m Staffel.

Gli atleti statunitensi sono stati i migliori nelle gare di staffetta. Hanno ghermito loro nella 4 x 100m (sotto) e nello stesso giorno potevano celebrare la vittoria nella 4 x 400m.

La finale du tournoi de football fut dominée par l'Allemagne de l'Est qui battit la Pologne 3:1.

East Germany dominated the football final, beating Poland by a score of 3:1.

Im Fussball-Endspiel dominierte die DDR gegen die Mannschaft aus Polen 3:1.

La finale di calcio fu vinta dalla Germania dell'est con 3:1 contro la Polonia.

Les marathoniens à travers
les rues de Montréal.
67 coureurs prirent le
départ de cette épreuve,
60 finirent la course.
Le vainqueur: Waldemar
Cierpinski, RDA.

The marathoners make their
way through the streets of
Montreal. Sixty-seven runners
began the contest and sixty
finished the course. Waldemar
Cierpinski of the GDR won.

Die Marathonläufer auf
ihrem Weg durch die Strassen
Montreals. 67 Läufer waren
am Start und 60 konnten
durchhalten. Waldemar
Cierpinski, DDR, siegte.

I maratoneti corrono per le
strade di Montreal. 67 atleti
iniziarono la gara ma solo 60
la terminavano. Il vincitore:
il tedesco orientale
Waldemar Cierpinski.

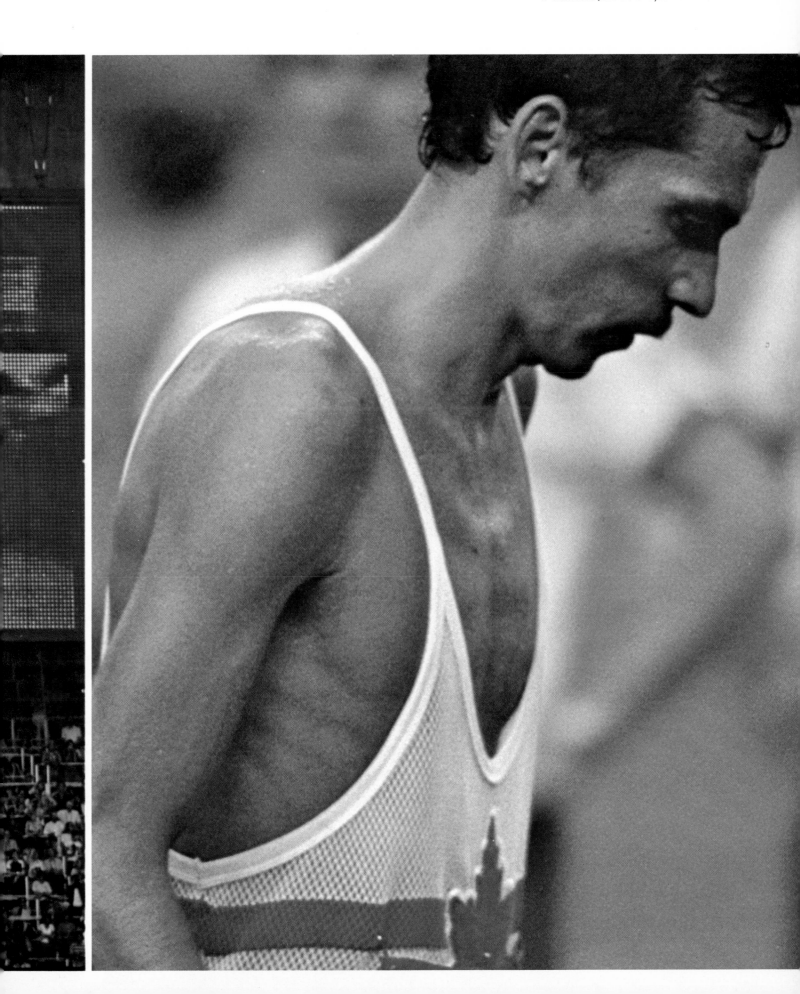

Jerome Drayton, Canada, termina sixième.

Canada's Jerome Drayton was sixth.

Jerome Drayton, Kanada, wurde Sechster.

Il canadese Jerome Drayton arrivato 6º.

L'équipe française fait ses adieux avec
l'or dans le Saut Grand Prix, tradition-
nellement la dernière épreuve des Olympiques.

The French team bid adieu with a gold in Grand Prix Jumping, traditionally the last event at the Olympics.

Die französische Equipe verabschiedet sich mit der Goldmedaille im Preis der Nationen, dem letzten Wettbewerb der Olympischen Spiele.

La squadra francese chiudeva in bellezza con una medaglia d'oro nel Gran Premio di salto, l'ultima gara delle olimpiadi.

LA CÉRÉMONIE DE CLÔTURE.

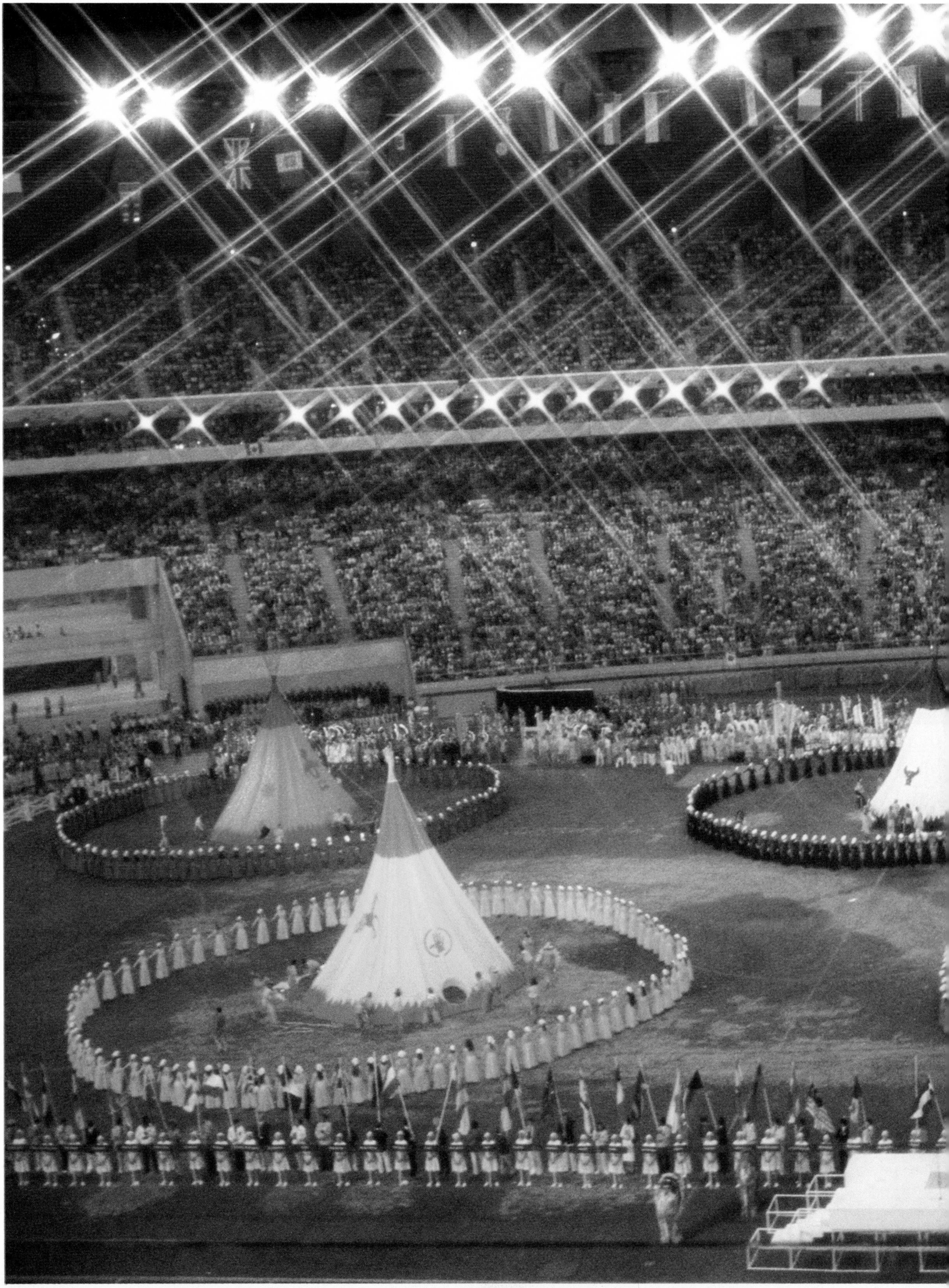

Les pays et leurs abréviations
The countries and their abbreviations
Die Länder und ihre Abkürzungen
I paesi e le loro abbreviazioni

	Français	English	Deutsch	Italiano
AFG	Afghanistan	Afghanistan	Afghanistan	Afganistan
AHO	Antilles néerlandaises	Netherlands Antilles	Niederländ Antillen	Antille Olandesi
ALB	Albanie	Albania	Albanien	Albania
ALG	Algérie	Algeria	Algerien	Algeria
ARG	Argentine	Argentina	Argentinien	Argentina
ARS	Arabie Saoudite	Saudi-Arabia	Saudi Arabien	Arabia Saudita
AUS	Australie	Australia	Australien	Australia
AUT	Autriche	Austria	Österreich	Austria
BAH	Bahamas	Bahamas	Bahamas	Bahama
BAR	Barbade	Barbados	Barbados	Barbados
BEL	Belgique	Belgium	Belgien	Belgio
BER	Bermudes	Bermuda	Bermuda	Bermude
BIR	Birmanie	Burma	Birma	Birmania
BIZ	Bélize	Belize	Belize	Belize
BOL	Bolivie	Bolivia	Bolivien	Bolivia
BRA	Brésil	Brazil	Brasilien	Brasile
BUL	Bulgarie	Bulgaria	Bulgarien	Bulgaria
CAN	Canada	Canada	Kanada	Canada
CGO	Congo	Congo	Kongo	Congo
CHA	Tchad	Chad	Tschad	Ciad
CHI	Chili	Chile	Chile	Cile
CIV	Côte-d'Ivoire	Ivory Coast	Elfenbeinküste	Costa d'Avorio
CMR	Cameroun	Cameroon	Kamerun	Cameroun
COL	Colombie	Columbia	Kolumbien	Colombia
CRC	Costa Rica	Costa Rica	Costa Rica	Costarica
CUB	Cuba	Cuba	Kuba	Cuba
DAH	Dahomey	Dahomey	Dahomey	Dahomey
DEN	Danemark	Denmark	Dänemark	Danimarca
DOM	Dominicaine (République)	Dominican Republic	Dominikanische Republik	Repubblica Dominicana
ECU	Equateur	Ecuador	Ecuador	Ecuador
EGY	Egypte	Egypt	Ägypten	Egitto
ESP	Espagne	Spain	Spanien	Spagna
ETH	Ethiopie	Ethiopia	Äthiopien	Etiopia
FIJ	Fidji (Iles)	Fiji Islands	Fidschi-Inseln	Isole Figi
FIN	Finlande	Finland	Finnland	Finlandia
FRA	France	France	Frankreich	Francia
GAB	Gabon	Gabon	Gabun	Gabon
GBR	Grande-Bretagne	Great Britain	Grossbritannien	Gran Bretagna
GDR	République démocratique allemande	German Democratic Republic	Deutsche Demokratische Republik	Repubblica Democratia Tedesca
GER	Allemagne	Germany	Deutschland	Germania
GHA	Ghana	Ghana	Ghana	Ghana
GRE	Grèce	Greece	Griechenland	Grecia
GUA	Guatemala	Guatemala	Guatemala	Guatemala
GUI	Guinée	Guinea	Guinea	Guinea
GUY	Guyane	Guyana	Guyana	Guiana
HAI	Haïti	Haiti	Haiti	Haiti
HKG	Hong-Kong	Hong Kong	Hongkong	Hong Kong
HOL	Pays-Bas	Netherlands	Niederlande	Paesi Bassi
HON	Honduras	Honduras	Honduras	Honduras

	Français	English	Deutsch	Italiano
HUN	Hongrie	Hungary	Ungarn	Ungheria
INA	Indonésie	Indonesia	Indonesien	Indonesia
IND	Inde	India	Indien	India
IRL	Irlande	Ireland	Irland	Irlanda
IRN	Iran	Iran	Iran	Iran
IRQ	Irak	Iraq	Irak	Iraq
ISL	Islande	Iceland	Island	Islanda
ISR	Israël	Israel	Israel	Israele
ISV	Vierges (Iles)	Virgin Islands	Jungfern-Inseln	Isole delle Vergini
ITA	Italie	Italy	Italien	Italia
JAM	Jamaïque	Jamaica	Jamaica	Giamaica
JOR	Jordanie	Jordan	Jordanien	Giordania
JPN	Japon	Japan	Japan	Giappone
KEN	Kenya	Kenya	Kenia	Kenia
KHM	Cambodge	Cambodia	Kambodscha	Cambogia
KOR	Corée	Korea	Korea	Corea
KUW	Koweït	Kuwait	Kuwait	Kuwait
LBA	Libye	Libya	Libyen	Libia
LES	Lesotho	Lesotho	Lesotho	Lesotho
LIB	Liban	Lebanon	Libanon	Libano
LIE	Liechtenstein	Liechtenstein	Liechtenstein	Liechtenstein
LUX	Luxembourg	Luxembourg	Luxemburg	Lussemburgo
MAD	Madagascar	Madagascar	Madagaskar	Madagascar
MAL	Malaisie	Malaysia	Malaysia	Malaysia
MAR	Maroc	Morocco	Marokko	Marocco
MAW	Malawi	Malawi	Malawi	Malawi
MEX	Mexique	Mexico	Mexico	Messico
MGL	Mongolie	Mongolia	Mongolei	Mongolia
MLI	Mali	Mali	Mali	Mali
MLT	Malte	Malta	Malta	Malta
MON	Monaco	Monaco	Monaco	Monaco
MRI	Maurice (Ile)	Mauritius	Mauritien	Maurizio
NCA	Nicaragua	Nicaragua	Nicaragua	Nicaragua
NEP	Népal	Nepal	Nepal	Nepal
NGR	Nigéria	Nigeria	Nigeria	Nigeria
NIG	Niger	Niger	Niger	Niger
NOR	Norvège	Norway	Norwegen	Norvegia
NGY	Papouasie-Nouvelle-Guinée	Papua-New Guinea	Papua-Neu Guinea	Papua-Nuova Guinea
NZL	Nouvelle-Zélande	New Zealand	Neuseeland	Nuova Zelanda
PAK	Pakistan	Pakistan	Pakistan	Pakistan
PAN	Panama	Panama	Panama	Panama
PAR	Paraguay	Paraguay	Paraguay	Paraguay
PER	Pérou	Peru	Peru	Peru
PHI	Philippines	Philippines	Philippinen	Filippine
POL	Pologne	Poland	Polen	Polonia
POR	Portugal	Portugal	Portugal	Portogallo
PRK	RDP Corée	DPR Korea	VR Korea	RDP Corea
PUR	Porto Rico	Puerto-Rico	Puerto Rico	Portorico
ROM	Roumanie	Rumania	Rumänien	Romania
SAL	Salvador (El)	El Salvador	El Salvador	El Salvador
SEN	Sénégal	Senegal	Senegal	Senegal
SIN	Singapour	Singapore	Singapur	Singapore
SLE	Sierra Leone	Sierra Leone	Sierra Leone	Sierra Leone
SMR	Saint-Marin	San Marino	San Marino	San Marino
SOM	Somalie	Somalia	Somalia	Somalia
SRI	Sri Lanka	Sri Lanka	Sri Lanka	Sri Lanka
SUD	Soudan	Sudan	Sudan	Sudan
SUI	Suisse	Switzerland	Schweiz	Svizzera
SUR	Surinam	Surinam	Surinam	Suriname
SWE	Suède	Sweden	Schweden	Svezia
SWZ	Souaziland	Swaziland	Swaziland	Swaziland
SYR	Syrie	Syria	Syrien	Siria

	Français	English	Deutsch	Italiano
TAN	Tanzanie	Tanzania	Tansania	Tanzania
TCH	Tchécoslovaquie	Czechoslovakia	Tschechoslowakei	Cecoslovacchia
THA	Thaïlande	Thailand	Thailand	Tailandia
TOG	Togo	Togo	Togo	Togo
TRI	Trinidad et Tobago	Trinidad and Tobago	Trinidad und Tobago	Trinidad e Tobago
TUN	Tunisie	Tunisia	Tunesien	Tunisia
TUR	Turquie	Turkey	Türkei	Turchia
UGA	Ouganda	Uganda	Uganda	Uganda
URS	U.R.S.S.	USSR	UdSSR	URSS
URU	Uruguay	Uruguay	Uruguay	Uruguay
USA	Etats-Unis	USA	USA	Stati Uniti
VEN	Venezuela	Venezuela	Venezuela	Venezuela
VNM	Viêt-nam	Viet-Nam	Vietnam	Vietnam
VOL	Haute-Volta	Upper Volta	Obervolta	Alto Volta
YUG	Yougoslavie	Yugoslavia	Jugoslawien	Iugoslavia
ZAI	Zaïre	Zaire	Zaire	Zaire
ZAM	Zambie	Zambia	Zambia	Zambia

Athlétisme
Athletics
Leichtathletik
Atletica leggera

1976 07-23/07-31

Dames   Ladies   Damen   Donne

100 m

1	Annegret Richter	GER		11.08
2	Renate Stecher	GDR		11.13
3	Inge Helten	GER		11.17
4	Raelene Boyle	AUS		11.23
5	Evelyn Ashford	USA		11.24
6	Chandra Cheeseborough	USA		11.31
—	Patty Loverock	CAN		11.40

200 m

1	Bärbel Eckert	GDR	RO/OR	22.37
2	Annegret Richter	GER		22.39
3	Renate Stecher	GDR		22.47
4	Carla Bodendorf	GDR		22.64
5	Inge Helten	GER		22.68
6	Tatyana Prorochenko	URS		23.03
—	Patty Loverock	CAN		23.09

400 m

1	Irena Szewinska	POL	RM/WR	49.29
2	Christina Brehmer	GDR		50.51
3	Ellen Streidt	GDR		50.55
4	Pirjo Haggman	FIN		50.56
5	Rosalyn Bryant	USA		50.65
6	Shelia Ingram	USA		50.90
—	Margaret Stride	CAN		53.14

800 m

1	Tatiana Kazankina	URS	RM/WR	1:54.94
2	Nikolina Chtereva	BUL		1:55.42
3	Elfi Zinn	GDR		1:55.60
4	Anita Weiss	GDR		1:55.74
5	Svetlana Styrkina	URS		1:56.44
6	Svetla Zlateva	BUL		1:57.21
—	Yvonne Saunders	CAN		2:03.54

1500 m

1	Tatiana Kazankina	URS	4:05.48
2	Gunhild Hoffmeister	GDR	4:06.02
3	Ulrike Klapezynski	GDR	4:06.09
4	Nikolina Chtereva	BUL	4:06.57
5	Liudmila Bragina	URS	4:07.20
6	Gabriell Dorio	ITA	4:07.27
—	Thelma Wright	CAN	4:15.23

100 m Haies/Hurdles/Hürden/Ostacoli

1	Johanna Schaller	GDR	12.77
2	Tatiana Anisimova	URS	12.78
3	Natalia Lebedeva	URS	12.80
4	Gudrun Berend	GDR	12.82
5	Grazyna Rabsztyn	POL	12.96
6	Esther Rot	ISR	13.04
—	Susan Bradley	CAN	14.07

4 x 100 m Relais   Relay   Staffel   Staffetta

1	Marlis Oelsner/Renate Stecher/Carla Bodendorf/Bärbel Eckert	GDR	RO/OR	42.55
2	Elvira Posseckel/Inge Helten/Annegret Richter/Annegret Kroniger	GER		42.59
3	Tatyana Prorochenko/Liudmila Maslakova/Nadezhda Besfamilnaya/Vera Anisimova	URS		43.09
4	Margaret Howe/Patty Loverock/Joanne McTaggart/Marjorie Bailey	CAN		43.17
5	Barbara Wilson/Deborah Wells/Denise Robertson/Raelene Boyle	AUS		43.18
6	Leleith Hodges/Rose Allwood/Carol Cummings/Jacquel Pusey	JAM		43.24

4 x 400 m   Relais   Relay   Staffel   Staffetta

#			
1	Doris Maletzki/Brigitte Rohde/Ellen Streidt/Christina Brehmer	GDR	**RM/WR** 3:19.23
2	Debra Sapenter/Shelia Ingram/Pam Jiles/Rosalyn Bryant	USA	3:22.81
3	Inta Klimovocha/Lyudmila Aksenova/Natalia Sokolova/Nadezhda Ilyina	URS	3:24.24
4	Judith Canty/Verna Burnard/Charlene Rendina/Bethanie Nail	AUS	3:25.56
5	Claudia Steger/Dagmar Fuhrmann/Elke Barth/Rita Wilden	GER	3:25.71
6	Marika Lindholm/Pirjo Haggman/Mona-Lisa Pursiainen/Riitta Salin	FIN	3:25.87
8	Margaret Stride/Joyce Yakubowich/Rachelle Campbell/Yvonne Saunders	CAN	3:28.91

Lancement du disque	Discus throw	Diskus	Lancio del disco		
1	Evelin Schlaak	GDR	**RO/OR**	69,00
2	Maria Vergova	BUL		67,30
3	Gabriele Hinymann	GDR		66,84
4	Faina Melnik	URS		66,40
5	Sabine Engel	GDR		65,88
6	Argentina Menis	ROM		65,38
11	Jane Haist	CAN		59,74

Lancement du javelot	Javelin throw	Speerwurf	Lancio del giavellotto		
1	Ruth Fuchs	GDR	**RO/OR**	65,94
2	Marion Becker	GER		64,70
3	Kathryn Schmidt	USA		63,96
4	Jacqueline Hein	GDR		63,84
5	Sabine Sebrowski	GDR		63,08
6	Svetlana Babich	URS		59,42

Lancement du poids	Shot put	Kugelstossen	Lancio del peso		
1	Ivanka Christova	BUL	**RO/OR**	21,16
2	Nadejda Chijova	URS		20,96
3	Helena Fibingerova	TCH		20,67
4	Marianne Adam	GDR		20,55
5	Ilona Schoknecht	GDR		20,54
6	Margitta Droese	GDR		19,79
13	Lucette Moreau	CAN		15,48

Saut en hauteur	High jump	Hochsprung	Salto in alto		
1	Rosemarie Ackermann	GDR	**RO/OR**	1,93
2	Sara Simeoni	ITA		1,91
3	Yordanka Blagoeva	BUL		1,91
4	Maria Mracnova	TCH		1,89
5	Joni Huntley	USA		1,89
6	Tatyana Shlyahto	URS		1,87
10	Julie White	CAN		1,87

Saut en longueur	Long jump	Weitsprung	Salto in lungo	
1	Angela Voigt	GDR	6,72
2	Kathy McMillan	USA	6,66
3	Lidiya Alfeeva	URS	6,60
11	Diane Jones	CAN	6,13
4	Siegrun Siegl	GDR	6,59
5	Ildiko Szabo	HUN	6,57
6	Jarmila Nygrynova	TCH	6,54

Pentathlon   Pentathlon   Fünfkampf   Pentathlon

			100 m Haies Hurdles Hürden Ostacoli	Poids Shot Put Kugel Peso	Hauteur High jump Hochsprung Salto alto	Longueur Long jump Weitsprung Salto lungo	200 m	
1	Siegrun Siegl	GDR	13.31 957	12,92 775	1,74 974	6,49 1012	23.09 1027	4745
2	Christine Laser	GDR	13.55 925	14,29 855	1,78 1012	6,27 965	23.48 988	4745
3	Burglinde Pollak	GDR	13.30 959	16,25 963	1,64 875	6,30 971	23.64 972	4740
4	Liudmi la Popovskaya	URS	13.33 955	15,02 896	1,74 974	6,19 947	24.10 928	4700
5	Nadejda Tkachenko	URS	13.41 944	14,90 889	1,80 1031	6,08 924	24.61 881	4669
6	Diane Jones	CAN	13.79 893	14,58 871	1,80 1031	6,29 969	25.33 818	4582

Athlétisme/Athletics/Leichtathletik/Atletica leggera

Messieurs   Men   Herren   Uomini

100 m

1	Hasely Crawford	TRI	10.06
2	Donald Quarrie	JAM	10.08
3	Valeriy Borzov	URS	10.14
4	Harvey Glance	USA	10.19
5	Gay Abrahams	PAN	10.25
6	John Jones	USA	10.27
—	Marvin Nash	CAN	10.52

200 m

1	Donald Quarrie	JAM	20.23
2	Millard Hampton	USA	20.29
3	Dwayne Evans	USA	20.43
4	Pietro Mennea	ITA	20.54
5	Ruy Da Silva	BRA	20.84
6	Bogdan Grzejszczak	POL	20.91
—	Hugh Fraser	CAN	21.57

400 m

1	Alberto Juantorena	CUB		44.26
2	Fred Newhouse	USA		44.40
3	Herman Frazier	USA		44.95
4	Alfons Brijdenbach	BEL		45.04
5	Maxie Parks	USA		45.24
6	Richard Mitchell	AUS		45.40
—	Brian Saunders	CAN		46.46

800 m

1	Alberto Juantorena	CUB	RM/WR	1:43.50
2	Ivo Vandamme	BEL		1:43.86
3	Richard Wohlhuter	USA		1:44.12
4	Willi Wülbeck	GER		1:45.26
5	Steven O'Vett	GBR		1:45.44
6	Lucijano Susanj	YUG		1:45.75

1500 m

1	John Walker	NZL	3:39.17
2	Ivo Vandamme	BEL	3:39.27
3	Paul-H. Wellmann	GER	3:39.33
4	Eamonn Coghlan	IRL	3:39.51
5	Frank Clement	GBR	3:39.65
6	Richard Wohlhuter	USA	3:40.64
—	Paul Craig	CAN	3:41.02

5000 m

1	Lasse Viren	FIN	13:24.76
2	Dick Quax	NZL	13:25.16
3	Klaus-P. Hildenbrand	GER	13:25.38
4	Rod Dixon	NZL	13:25.50
5	Brendan Foster	GBR	13:26.19
6	Willy Polleunis	BEL	13:26.99
—	Grant McLaaren	CAN	13:46.40

10 000 m

1	Lasse Viren	FIN	27:40.38
2	Carlos Sousa Lopes	POR	27:45.17
3	Brendan Foster	GBR	27:54.92
4	Anthony Simmons	GBR	27:56.26
5	Ilie Floroiu	ROM	27:59.93
6	Mariano Harocisneros	ESP	28:00.28
—	Dan Shaughnessy	CAN	29:26.96

20 km   Marche   Walk   Gehen   Marcia

1	Daniel Bautista	MEX	1,24:40.6
2	Hans Reimann	GDR	1,25:13.8
3	Peter Frenkel	GDR	1,25:29.4
4	Karl-Heinz Stadtmüller	GDR	1,26:50.6
5	Raul Gonzalez	MEX	1,28:18.2
6	Armando Zanbaldo	ITA	1,28:25.2
—	Marcel Jobin	CAN	1,34:33.4

Marathon 42,195 km

1	Waldemar Cierpinska	GDR	2,09:55.0
2	Frank Shorter	USA	2,10:45.8
3	Karel Lismont	BEL	2,11:12.6
4	Donald Kardong	USA	2,11:15.8
5	Lasse Viren	FIN	2,13:10.8
6	Jerome Drayton	CAN	2,13:30.0

3000 m   Steeplechase   Hindernis   Siepi

1	Anders Garderud	SWE	RM/WR	8:08.02
2	Bronisla Malinowski	POL		8:09.11
3	Frank Baumgartl	GDR		8:10.36
4	Tapio Kantanen	FIN		8:12.60
5	Michael Karst	GER		8:20.14
6	Evan Robertson	NZL		8:21.08

110 m   Haies   Hurdles   Hürden   Ostacoli

1	Guy Drut	FRA	13.30
2	Alejandro Casanas	CUB	13.33
3	Willie Davenport	USA	13.38
4	Charles Foster	USA	13.41
5	Thomas Munkelt	GDR	13.44
6	James Owens	USA	13.73
—	Daniel Taillon	CAN	14.23

400 m   Haies   Hurdles   Hürden   Ostacoli

1	Edwin Moses	USA	RM/WR	47.64
2	Michael Shine	USA		48.69
3	Evgeniy Gavrilenko	URS		49.45
4	Quentin Wheeler	USA		49.86
5	Jose Jesus Carvalho	POR		49.94
6	Yanko Bratanov	BUL		50.03

4 x 100 m   Relais   Relay   Staffel   Staffetta

1	Harvey Glance/John Jones/Millard Hampton/Steven Riddick	USA	38.33
2	Manfred Kokot/Jorg Pfeifer/Dieter Kurrat/Alesander Thieme	GDR	38.66
3	Alesander Aksinin/Nikolai Kolesnikov/Yuriy Silov/Valeriy Borzov	URS	38.78
4	Andrzej Swierczynski/Marian Woronin/Bogdan Grzejszczak/Zenon Licznerski	POL	38.83
5	Francisco Gomez/Alejandro Casanas/Hermes Ramirez/Silvio Leonard	CUB	39.01
6	Vincenzo Guerini/Luciano Caravani/Luigi Benedetti/Pietro Mennea	ITA	39.08
8	Hugh Spooner/Marvin Nash/Albin Dukowski/Hugh Fraser	CAN	39.47

4 x 400 m   Relais   Relay   Staffel   Staffetta

1	Herman Frazier/Benjamin Brown/Fred Newhouse/Maxie Parks	USA	2:58.65
2	Ryszard Podlas/Jan Werner/Zbigniew Jaremski/Jerzy Pietrzyk	POL	3:01.43
3	Franz-P. Hofmeister/Lothar Krieg/Harald Schmid/Bernd Herrmann	GER	3:01.98
4	Ian Seale/Don Domansky/Leighton Hope/Brian Saunders	CAN	3:02.64
5	Leighton Priestley/Donald Quarrie/Colin Bradford/Seymour Newman	JAM	3:02.84
6	Michael Solomon/Horace Tuitt/Joseph Coombs/Charles Joseph	TRI	3:03.46

Lancement du disque — Discus throw — Diskus — Lancio del disco

1	Mac Wilkins	USA		67,50
2	Wolfgang Schmidt	GDR		66,22
3	John Powell	USA		65,70
4	Norbert Thiede	GDR		64,30
5	Siegfried Pachale	GDR		64,24
6	Pentti Kahma	FIN		63,12
—	Ain Roost	CAN		56,56

Lancement du marteau — Hammer throw — Hammerwerfen — Lancio del martello

1	Yuriy Sedyh	URS	RO/OR	77,52
2	Alexey Spiridonov	URS		76,08
3	Anatoliy Bondarchuk	URS		75,48
4	Karl-H. Riehm	GER		75,46
5	Walter Schmidt	GER		74,72
6	Jochen Sachse	GDR		74,30
—	Murray Keating	CAN		65,68

Lancement du javelot — Javelin throw — Speerwurf — Lancio del giavellotto

1	Miklos Nemeth	HUN	RM/WR	94,58
2	Hannu Siitonen	FIN		87,92
3	Gheorghe Megelea	ROM		87,16
4	Piotr Bielczyk	POL		86,50
5	Sam Colson	USA		86,16
6	Vasiliy Ershov	URS		85,26
—	Philip Olsen	CAN		77,70

Lancement du poids — Shot put — Kugelstossen — Lancio del peso

1	Udo Beyer	GDR	21,05
2	Evgeni Mironov	URS	21,03
3	Alexander Barisnikov	URS	21,00
4	Allan Feuerbach	USA	20,55
5	Hans-Peter Gies	GDR	20,47
6	Geoffrey Capes	GBR	20,36
—	Bruce Pirnie	CAN	17,82

Saut à la perche — Pole vault — Stabhochsprung — Salto con l'asta

1	Tadeusz Slusarski	POL	RO/OR	5,50
2	Antti Kalliomaki	FIN		5,50
3	David Roberts	USA		5,50
4	Patrick Abada	FRA		5,45
5	Wojciech Buciarski	POL		5,45
6	Earl Bell	USA		5,45
—	Bruce Simpson	CAN		*aucune hauteur/no height*

Saut en hauteur — High jump — Hochsprung — Salto in alto

1	Jacek Wszola	POL	RO/OR	2,25
2	Greg Joy	CAN		2,23
3	Dwight Stones	USA		2,21
4	Sergey Budalov	URS		2,21
5	Sergey Seniukov	URS		2,18
6	Rodolfo Bergamo	ITA		2,18
12.	Claude Ferragne	CAN		2,14

Saut en longueur — Long jump — Weitsprung — Salto in lungo

1	Arnie Robinson	USA	8,35
2	Randy Williams	USA	8,11
3	Frank Wartenberg	GDR	8,02
4	Jacques Rousseau	FRA	8,00
	Joao de Oliviera	BRA	8,00
6	Nenad Stekic	YUG	7,89
—	Richard Rock	CAN	7,57

Triple saut — Triple jump — Dreisprung — Salto triplo

1	Victor Saneev	URS	17,29
2	James Butts	USA	17,18
3	Joao de Oliviera	BRA	16,90
4	Pedro Perez	CUB	16,81
5	Tommy Haynes	USA	16,78
6	Wolfgang Kolmsee	GER	16,68

Décathlon — Decathlon — Zehnkampf — Decathlon

			100 m	Longueur / Long jump / Weitspr. / Lungo	Poids / S. Put / Kugel / Peso	Hauteur / High jump / Hochspr. / Alto	400 m	110 m Haies / Hurd. / Hurd. / Osta.	Disque / Discus / Diskus / Disco	Perche / Pole vault / Stabhoch. / Asta	Javelot / Javelin / Speer / Giavel.	1500 m		
1	Bruce Jenner	USA	10.94	7,22	15,35	2,03	47.51	14.84	50,04	4,80	68,52	4:12.61		
			819	865	809	882	923	866	873	1005	862	714	RM/WR	8618
2	Guido Kratschmer	GER	10.66	7,39	14,74	2,03	48.19	14.58	45,70	4,60	66,32	4:29.09		
			890	899	773	882	889	895	794	957	837	595		8411
3	Nikolay Avilov	URS	11.23	7,52	14,81	2,14	48.16	14.20	45,60	4,45	62,28	4:26.26		
			749	925	777	975	889	939	792	920	789	614		8369
4	Raimo Pihl	SWE	10.93	6,99	15,55	2,00	47.97	15.81	44,30	4,40	77,34	4:28.76		
			822	818	821	857	898	767	768	909	961	597		8218
5	Ryszard Skowronek	POL	11.02	7,26	13,74	1,91	47.91	14.75	45,34	4,80	62,22	4:29.89		
			799	873	712	779	903	876	788	1005	788	590		8113
6	Siegfried Stark	GDR	11.35	6,98	15,08	1,91	49.14	15.65	45,48	4,65	74,18	4:24.93		
			721	816	793	779	847	782	790	969	926	625		8048

Aviron/Rowing/Rudern/Canottaggio

Dames   Ladies   Damen   Donne

1000 m   Une rameuse   Single sculls   Einer   Singolo

1	Christine Scheiblich	GDR	4:05.56		4	Rossitza Spassova	BUL	4:10.86
2	Joan Lind	USA	4:06.21		5	Ingrid Munneke	HOL	4:18.71
3	Elena Antonova	URS	4:10.24		6	Mariann Ambrus	HUN	4:22.59
11	Colette Pepin	CAN	4:34.76					

1000 m   Deux en couple   Double sculls   1000 m   Deux en pointe sans barreur   Pair without coxswain
Doppelzweier   Due di coppia   Zweier ohne Steuermann   Due senza timoniere

1	Svetla Otzetova / Zdravka Yordanova	BUL	3:44.36	1	Siika Kelbetcheva / Stoyanka Grouitcheva	BUL	4:01.22
2	Sabine Jahn / Petra Bösler	GDR	3:47.86	2	Angelika Noack / Sabine Dahne	GDR	4:01.64
3	Leonora Kaminskaite / Genovate Ramoshkene	URS	3:49.93	3	Edith Eckbauer / Thea Einöder	GER	4:02.35
4	Solfrid Johansen / Ingunn Brechan	NOR	3:52.18	4	Natalia Gorodilova / Anna Karnaushenko	URS	4:03.27
5	Jan Palchikoff / Diane Braceland	USA	3:58.25	5	Tricia Smith / Elisabeth Craig	CAN	4:08.09
6	Cheryl Howard / Bev Cameron	CAN	4:06.23	6	Marlena Predescu / Marinela Maxim	ROM	4:15.44

1000 m   Quatre en couple avec barreur   Four sculls with coxswain   Doppelvierer mit Steuermann   Quattro di coppia con timoniere

1	Anke Borchmann/Jutta Lau/Viola Poley/Roswietha Zobelt/Liane Weigelt	GDR	3:29.99
2	Anna Kondrachina/Mira Bryunina/Larisa Alexandrova/Galina Ermolaeva/Nadezhda Chernysheva	URS	3:32.49
3	Iona Tudoran/Maria Micsa/Felicia Afrasiloaia/Elisabe Lazar/Elena Giurca	ROM	3:32.76
4	Iskra Velinova/Verka Aleksieva/Trayanka Vassileva/Svetla Gintcheva/Stanka Gueorguieva	BUL	3:34.13
5	Anna Maresova/Marie Bartakova/Jarmila Patkova/Hana Kavkova/Alena Svobodova	TCH	3:42.53
6	Kirsten Thomsen/Else Maersk-Kristensen/Judith Andersen/Karen Nielsen/Kirsten Plum-Jensen	DEN	3:46.99
9	Sandra Kirby/Elaine Bourbeau/Guylaine Bernier/Barbara Boettcher/Johanne Delisle	CAN	3:57.72

1000 m   Quatre en pointe avec barreur   Four with coxswain   Vierer mit Steuermann   Quattro con timoniere

1	Karin Metze/Bianka Schwede/Gabriele Lohs/Andrea Kurth/Sabine Hess	GDR	3:45.08
2	Ginka Gurova/Liliana Vasseva/Reni Yordanova/Mariika Modeva/Kapka Gueorguieva	BUL	3:48.24
3	Nadezhda Sevostyanova/Lyudmila Krokhina/Galina Mishenina/Anna Pasokha/Lidiya Krylova	URS	3:49.38
4	Elena Oprea/Florica Petcu/Filigonia Tol/Aurelia Marinescu/Aneta Matei	ROM	3:51.17
5	Liesbeth Vosmaaer/Hette Borrias/Myriam von Rooyen/Ans Gravesteyn/Monique Pronk	HOL	3:54.36
6	Pamela Behrens/Catherin Menges/Nancy Storrs/Julia Geer/Mary Kellogg	USA	3:56.50
7	Linda Schaumleffel/Dolores Young/Monica Draeger/Joy Fera/Barbara Mutch	CAN	3:46.18

1000 m   Huit en pointe avec barreur   Eight with coxswain   Achter mit Steuermann   Otto con timoniere

1	Viola Goretzki/Christiane Knetsch/Ilona Richter/Brigitte Ahrenholz/Monika Kallies Henrietta Ebert/Helma Lehmann/Irina Müller/Marina Wilke	GDR	3:33.32
2	Lyubov Talalaeva/Nadezda Roshchina/Klavdiya Kozenkova/Elena Zubko/Olga Kolkova Nelli Tarakanova/Nadezhda Rozgon/Olga Guzenko/Olga Pugovskaya	URS	3:36.17
3	Jacqueli Zoch/Anita Defrantz/Carie Graves/Marion Greig/Anne Warner Peggy McCarthy/Carol Brown/Gail Ricketson/Lynn Silliman	USA	3:38.68
4	Carol Eastmore/Rhonda Ross/Nancy Higgins/Mazina Delure/Susan Antoft Wendy Pullan/Christine Neuland/Gail Cort/Illona Smith	CAN	3:39.52
5	Waltraud Roick/Erika Endriss/Monika Zipplies/Brigit Kiesow/Hiltrud Guertler Isolde Eisele/Marianne Weber/Eva Dick/Ingrid Huhn-Wagener	GER	3:41.06
6	Elena Oprea/Florica Petcu/Filigonia Tol/Aurelia Marinescu/Georgeta Militaru Iuliana Munteanu/Elena Avram/Marioara Constantin/Aneta Matei	ROM	3:44.79

Aviron/Rowing/Rudern/Canottaggio

Messieurs   Men   Herren   Uomini

2000 m   Un rameur   Single sculls   Einer   Singolo

1	Pertti Karpinnen	FIN	7:29.03		4	Sean Drea	IRL	7:42.53
2	Peter-M. Kolbe	GER	7:31.67		5	Nikolai Dovgan	URS	7:57.39
3	Joachim Dreifke	GDR	7:38.03		6	Ricardo Ibarra	ARG	8:03.05

2000 m	Deux en couple Doppelzweier	Double sculls Due di coppia			2000 m	Deux en pointe sans barreur Zweier ohne Steuermann	Pair without coxswain Due senza timoniere	
1	Frank Hansen Alf Hansen	NOR		7:13.20	1	Jörg Landvoigt Bernd Landvoigt	GDR	7:23.31
2	Chris Baillieu Michael Hart	GBR		7:15.26	2	Calvin Coffey Michael Staines	USA	7:26.73
3	Ulrich Schmied Jürgen Bertow	GDR		7:17.45	3	Peter Van Roye Thomas Strauss	GER	7:30.03
4	Yevgeni Barbakov Gennadi Korshikov	URS		7:18.87	4	Zlatko Celent Dusko Mrduljas	YUG	7:34.17
5	Peter Becker Gerhard Kroschewski	GER		7:22.15	5	Valentin Stoev Gueorgui Gueorguiev	BUL	7:37.42
6	Jean-Noel Ribot Jean-Michel Izart	FRA		7:50.18	6	Miroslav Knapek Vojtech Caska	TCH	7:51.06
					9	Brian Love Michael Neary	CAN	7:30.24 *finale/final 7-12*

2000 m	Deux en pointe avec barreur	Pair with coxswain	Zweier mit Steuermann	Due con timoniere		
1	Harald Jahrling/Friedrich Ulrich/Georg Spohr				GDR	7:58.99
2	Dmitri Bekhterev/Yuri Shurkalov/Yuri Lorentson				URS	8:01.82
3	Oldrich Svojanovsky/Pavel Svojanovsky/Ludvik Vebr				TCH	8:03.28
4	Roumen Christov/Tzvetan Petkov/Tocho Kichev				BUL	8:11.27
5	Primo Baran/Annibale Venier/Franco Venturini				ITA	8:15.97
6	Ryszard Stadniuk/Grzegorz Stellak/Ryszard Kubiak				POL	8:23.02
—	Robert Bergen/Walter Krawec/Michel Riendeau				CAN	*repêchage 1*

2000 m	Quatre en couple	Four sculls	Doppelvierer	Quattro di coppia		
1	Wolfgang Güldenpfennig/Rüdiger Reiche/K.-Heinz Bussert/Michael Wolfgramm				GDR	6:18.65
2	Yevgeny Duleev/Yuri Yakimov/Aivar Lazdenieks/Vitautas Butkus				URS	6:19.89
3	Jaroslav Helebrand/Vaclav Vochoska/Zdenek Pecka/Vladek Lacina				TCH	6:21.77
4	Norbert Kothe/Helmut Krause/Michael Gentsch/Helmut Wolber				GER	6:24.81
5	Yordan Valtchev/Mintcho Nicolov/Christo Jelev/Eftim Guerzilov				BUL	6:32.04
6	Peter Cortes/Kenneth Foote/Neil Halleen/John van Blom				USA	6:34.33
11	Louis Bourassa/York Langerfeld/Louis Prevost/André Renart				CAN	6:44.74

2000 m	Quatre en pointe sans barreur	Four without coxswain	Vierer ohne Steuermann	Quattro senza timoniere		
1	Siegfried Brietzke/Andreas Decker/Stefan Semmler/Wolfgang Mager				GDR	6:37.42
2	Ole Nafstad/Arne Bergodd/Finn Tveter/Rolf Andreassen				NOR	6:41.22
3	Raul Arnemann/Nikolai Kuznetsov/Valeri Dolinin/Anushavan Gasan-Dzhalalov				URS	6:42.52
4	Bob Murphy/Grant McAuley/Des Lock/David Lindstrom				NZL	6:43.23
5	Brian Dick/Philip Monckton/Andrew van Ruyven/Ian Gordon				CAN	6:46.11
6	Bernhard Foelkel/Klaus Roloff/Wolfgang Horak/Johann-G. Konertz				GER	6:47.44

2000 m	Quatre en pointe avec barreur	Four with coxswain	Vierer mit Steuermann	Quattro con timoniere		
1	Vladimir Eshinov/Nikolai Ivanov/Mikhail Kuznetsov/Alexandr Klepikov/Alexandr Lukianov				URS	6:40.22
2	Andreas Schulz/Rüdiger Kunze/Walter Diessner/Ullrich Diessner/Johannes Thomas				GDR	6:42.70
3	Johann Färber/Ralph Kubail/Siegfried Fricke/Peter Niehusen/Hartmut Wenzel				GER	6:46.96
4	Otakar Marecek/Karel Neffe/Milan Suchopar/Vladimir Janos/Vladimir Petricek				TCH	6:50.15
5	Lachezar Boitchev/Nasko Mintchev/Ivan Botev/Kiril Kirtchev/Nenko Dobrev				BUL	6:52.88
6	Viv Haar/Danny Keane/Tim Logan/Ian Boserio/David Simmons				NZL	7:00.17

2000 m	Huit en pointe avec barreur	Eight with coxswain	Achter mit Steuermann	Otto con timoniere		
1	Bernd Baumgart/Gottfried Dohn/Werner Klatt/Joachim Luck/Dieter Wendisch Roland Kostulski/Ulrich Karnatz/K.-Heins Prudohl/K.-Heinz Danielowski				GDR	5:58.29
2	Richard Lester/John Yallop/Timothy Crooks/Hugh Matheson/David Maxwell James Clark/Fred Smallbone/Leonard Robertson/Patrick Sweeney				GBR	6:00.82
3	Ivan Sutherland/Trevor Coker/Peter Dignan/Lindsay Wilson/Athol Earl Dave Rodger/Alex McLean/Tony Hurt/Simon Dickie				NZL	6:03.51
4	Reinhard Wendemuth/Bernd Truschinski/Frank Schütze/Frithjof Henckel/Wolfram Thiem Volker Sauer/Otmar Kaufhold/Wolf. Oschlies/Helmut Latz				GER	6:06.15
5	Islay Lee/Ian Clubb/Timothy Conrad/Robert Paver/Gary Eubergang Athol MacDonald/Peter Shakespear/Brian Richardson/Stuart Carter				AUS	6:09.75
6	Pavel Konvicka/Vaclav Mls/Josef Plaminek/Josef Pokorny/Karel Mejta Josef Nesticky/Lubomir Zapletal/Miroslav Vrastil/Jiri Ptak				TCH	6:14.29
8	Edgar Smith/Dirk Gidney/George Tintor/James Henniger/Patrick Croskerry Melvin La Forme/Ronald Burak/Alexander Manson/Robert Choquette				CAN	*finale/final 7-12* 6:09.03

Boxe/Boxing/Boxen/Pugilato

– 48 kg
Poids mi-mouche
Light flyweight
Halb-Fliegengewicht
Mosca leggeri

1	Jorge Hernandez	CUB
2	Byong Uk Li	PRK
3	Payao Pooltarat	THA
	Orlando Maldonado	PUR
—	Sidney McNight	CAN 1/16

– 51 kg
Poids mouche
Flyweight
Fliegengewicht
Mosca

1	Leo Randolph	USA
2	Ramon Duvalon	CUB
3	David Torosyan	URS
	Leszek Blazynski	POL
—	Ian Clyde	CAN 1/4

– 54 kg
Poids coq
Bantamweight
Bantamgewicht
Gallo

1	Yong Jo Gu	PRK
2	Charles Mooney	USA
3	Patrick Cowdell	GBR
	Victor Rybakov	URS
—	Chris Ius	CAN 1/8

– 57 kg
Poids plume
Featherweight
Federgewicht
Piuma

1	Angel Herrera	CUB
2	Richard Nowakowski	GDR
3	Leszek Kosedowski	POL
	Juan Paredes	MEX
—	Camille Huard	CAN 1/8

– 60 kg
Poids léger
Lightweight
Leichtgewicht
Leggeri

1	Howard Davis	USA
2	Simion Cutov	ROM
3	Vasily Solomin	URS
	Ace Rusevski	YUG

– 63.5 kg
Poids mi-welter
Light welterweight
Halbweltergewicht
Welter leggeri

1	Ray Leonard	USA
2	Andres Aldama	CUB
3	Vladimir Kolev	BUL
	Kazimier Szczerba	POL
—	Chris Clarke	CAN 1/8

– 67 kg
Poids welter
Welterweight
Weltergewicht
Welter

1	Jochen Bachfeld	GDR
2	Pedro Gamarro	VEN
3	Reinhard Skricek	GER
	Victor Zilberman	ROM
—	Carmen Rinke	CAN 1/4

– 71 kg
Poids sur-welter
Light middleweight
Halbmittelgewicht
Welter pesanti

1	Jerzy Rybicki	POL
2	Tadija Kacar	YUG
3	Victor Savchenko	URS
	Rolando Garbey	CUB
—	Michel Prevost	CAN 1/16

– 75 kg
Poids moyen
Middleweight
Mittelgewicht
Medi

1	Michael Spinks	USA
2	Rufat Riskiev	URS
3	Alec Nastac	ROM
	Luis Martinez	CUB
—	Bryan Gibson	CAN 1/16

– 81 kg
Poids mi-lourd
Light heavyweight
Halbschwergewicht
Medio massimi

1	Leon Spinks	USA
2	Sixto Soria	CUB
3	Costica Dafinoiu	ROM
	Janusz Gortat	POL
—	Roger Fortin	CAN 1/16

+ 81 kg
Poids lourd
Heavyweight
Schwergewicht
Massimo

1	Teofilo Stevenson	CUB
2	Mircea Simon	ROM
3	Johnny Tate	USA
	Clarence Hill	BER

Canoë/Canoeing/Kanu/Canoa

Dames   **Ladies**   **Damen**   **Donne**

Kayak-1   500 m

1	Carola Zirzow	GDR	2:01.05
2	Tatiana Korshunova	URS	2:03.07
3	Klara Rajnai	HUN	2:05.01
4	Ewa Kaminska	POL	2:05.16
5	Maria Mihoreanu	ROM	2:05.40
6	Anastazie Hajna	TCH	2:06.72
—	Susan Holloway	CAN	2:13.23

Kayak-2   500 m

1	Nina Gopova / Galina Kreft	URS	1:51.15
2	Anna Pfeffer / Klara Rajnai	HUN	1:51.69
3	Bärbel Köster / Carola Zirzow	GDR	1:51.81
4	Nastasia Nichitov / Agafia Orlov	ROM	1:53.77
5	Barbara Lewe-Pohlmann / Heide Wallbaum	GER	1:53.86
6	Maria Kazanecka / Katarzyn Kulizak	POL	1:55.05
8	Anne Dodge / Susan Holloway	CAN	1:56.75

Messieurs   **Men**   **Herren**   **Uomini**

Kayak-1   500 m

1	Vasile Diba	ROM	1:46.41
2	Zoltan Sztanity	HUN	1:46.95
3	Rüdiger Helm	GDR	1:48.30
4	Herminio Menendez	ESP	1:48.40
5	Grzegorz Sledziewski	POL	1:48.49
6	Sergey Lizunov	URS	1:49.21
—	Dean Oldershaw	CAN	1:54.88

Canadien/Canadian-1   500 m

1	Aleksandr Rogov	URS	1:59.23
2	John Wood	CAN	1:59.58
3	Matija Ljubek	YUG	1:59.60
4	Borislav Ananiev	BUL	1:59.92
5	Wilfried Stephan	GDR	2:00.54
6	Karoly Szegedi	HUN	2:01.12

Kayak-2		500 m		
1	Joachim Mattern Bernd Olbricht	GDR		1:35.87
2	Sergey Nagorny Vladimir Romanovskiy	URS		1:36.81
3	Larion Serghei Policarp Malihin	ROM		1:37.43
4	Jose Seguin Guiller del Riego	ESP		1:38.50
5	Jozsef Deme Janos Ratkai	HUN		1:38.81
6	Hannu Kojo Kari Markkanen	FIN		1:39.59
—	Denis Barre Steve King	CAN		1:41.47

Kayak-1		1000 m		
1	Rüdiger Helm	GDR		3:48.20
2	Geza Csapo	HUN		3:48.84
3	Vasile Diba	ROM		3:49.65
4	Oreste Perri	ITA		3:51.13
5	Aleksandr Shaparenko	URS		3:51.45
6	Berndt Andersson	SWE		3:52.46
—	Reed Oldershaw	CAN	*demi-finale/semi-final*	

Kayak-2		1000 m		
1	Sergey Nagorny Vladimir Romanovskiy	URS		3:29.01
2	Joachim Mattern Bernd Olbricht	GDR		3:29.33
3	Zoltan Bako Istvan Szabo	HUN		3:30.36
4	Jean-Paul Hanquier Alain Lebas	FRA		3:33.05
5	Guiller del Riego Jose Sequin	ESP		3:33.16
6	Jean-Pierre Burny Paul Hoekstra	BEL		3:33.86
8	Steve King, Denis Barre	CAN		3:34.46

Canadien/Canadian-2		500 m		
1	Sergej Petrenko Aleksandr Vinogradov	URS		1:45.81
2	Jerzy Opara Andrzej Gronowicz	POL		1:47.77
3	Tamas Buday Oszkar Frey	HUN		1:48.35
4	Gheorghe Danielov Gheorghe Simionov	ROM		1:48.84
5	François Millot Gérald Delacroix	FRA		1:49.74
6	Ivan Bourtchin Krassimi Christov	BUL		1:50.43
7	Gregory Smith John Wood	CAN		1:50.74

Canadien/Canadian-1		1000 m		
1	Matija Ljubek	YUG		4:09.51
2	Vasiliy Urchenko	URS		4:12.57
3	Tamas Wichmann	HUN		4:14.11
4	Borislav Ananiev	BUL		4:14.41
5	Ivan Patzaichin	ROM		4:15.08
6	Roland Iché	FRA		4:18.23
9	John Edwards	CAN		4:30.55

Canadien/Canadian-2		1000 m		
1	Sergej Petrenko Aleksandr Vinogradov	URS		3:52.76
2	Gheorghe Danielov Gheorghe Simionov	ROM		3:54.28
3	Tamas Buday Oszkar Frey	HUN		3:55.66
4	Jerzy Opara Andrzej Gronowicz	POL		3:59.56
5	Dettlef Bothe H.-Juergen Tode	GDR		4:00.37
6	Jiri Ctvrtecka Tomas Sach	TCH		4:01.48
—	Jeremy Abbott, John Edwards	CAN *repêchage/repechage*	3:54.33	

Kayak-4		1000 m		
1	Sergey Chuhray/Aleksandr Degtiarev/Yuriy Filatov/Vlademir Morozov		URS	3:08.69
2	Jose Celorrio/Jose Diaz-Flor/Herminio Menendez/Luis Misione		ESP	3:08.95
3	Peter Bischof/Bernd Duvigneau/Rüdiger Helm/Jürgen Lehnert		GDR	3:10.76
4	Nicusor Eseanu/Vasile Simiocenco/Neculai Simionenco/Mihai Zafiu		ROM	3:11.35
5	Henryk Budzicz/Kazimier Gorecki/Grzegorz Koltan/Ryszard Oborski		POL	3:12.17
6	Morten Mörland/Einar Rasmussen/Olaf Söyland/Jostein Stige		NOR	3:12.28
—	Hugh Fisher/Jean Fournel/Peter Patasi/Lou Tollas		CAN	3:14.49

Cyclisme/Cycling/Radsport/Ciclismo

1976					07-18/07-26

Messieurs	Men	Herren	Uomini		

180 km	Epreuve individuelle sur route Strassenrennen Einzelwertung		Individual road race Gara in circuito chiuso individuale		
1	Bernt Johansson	SWE	37,648 km/h	4,46:52.0
2	Giuseppe Martinelli	ITA		4,47:23.0
3	Mieczysl Nowicki	POL		4,47:23.0
4	Alfons de Wolf	BEL		4,47:23.0
5	Nikolai Gorelov	URS		4,47:23.0
6	George Mount	USA		4,47:23.0
24	Pierre Harvey	CAN		4,50:07.0

1000 m	Contre la montre Zeitfahren		Time trial Cors a cronometro		
1	Klaus-Jürgen Grünke	GDR	54,606 km/h	1:05.927
2	Michel Vaarten	BEL		1:07.516
3	Niels Fredborg	DEN		1:07.617
4	Janusz Kierzkowski	POL		1:07.660
5	Erick Vermeulen	FRA		1:07.846
6	Hans Michalsky	GER		1:07.878
13	Jocelyn Lovell	CAN		1:08.852

1000 m	Vitesse Sprint	Sprint Velocità		
1	Anton Tkac	TCH		11.17 3R
2	Daniel Morelon	FRA		
3	Hans-Jürgen Geschke	GDR		11.42 3R
4	Dieter Berkmann	GER		
5	Sergey Kravtsov	URS		
6	Yoshika Cho	JPN		
—	Gordon Singleton	CAN		

4000 m	Poursuite individuelle Einzel-Verfolgungsfahren	Individual pursuit Corsa inseguimento individuale		
1	Gregor Braun	GER	50,068 km/h	4:47.61
2	Herman Ponsteen	HOL		4:49.72
3	Thomas Huschke	GDR		4:52.71
4	Vladimir Osokin	URS		4:57.34
5	Orfeo Pizzoferrato	ITA		
6	Garry Sutton	AUS		

4000 m	Pursuite par équipe　Team pusuit　Mannschafts-Verfolgungsfahren　Corso inseguimento a squadra		
1	Gregor Braun/Hans Lutz/Gunther Schumacher,/Peter Vonhof	GER 55,160 km/h	4:21.06
2	Vladimir Osokin/Alexandr Perov/Vitaly Petrakov/Victor Sokolov	URS	4:27.15
3	Ian Banbury/Michael Bennett/Robin Croker/Ian Hallam	GBR	4:22.41
4	Norbert Durpisch/Thomas Huschke/Uwe Unterwalder/Matthias Wiegand	GDR	4:22.75
—	Ron Hayman/Jocelyn Lovell/Adrian Prosser/Hugh Walton	CAN	4:31.90

100 km	Contre la montre par équipe　Team time trial　Mannschafts-Zeitfahren　Corsa squadra a cronometro		
1	Anatoly Shukanov/Valery Shaplygin/Vladimir Kaminsky/Aavo Pikkuus	URS	2,08:53.0
2	Tadeusz Mytnik/Mieczysl Nowicki/Stanisla Szozda/Ryszard Szurkowski	POL	2,09:13.0
3	Verner Blaudzun/Gert Frank/Jorgen Hansen/Jorn Lund	DEN	2,12:20.0
4	Hans-Peter Jakst/Olaf Paltian/Friedrich von Löffelholz/Peter Weibel	GER	2,12:35.0
5	Petr Buchacek/Petr Matousek/Milan Puzrla/Vladimir Vondracek	TCH	2,12:56.0
6	Paul Carbutt/Philip Griffiths/Dudley Hayton/William Nickson	GBR	2,13:10.0
16	Mard Blouin/Brian Chewter/Tom Morris/Serge Proulx	CAN	2,17:15.0

Escrime/Fencing/Fechten/Scherma

1976　　　　　　　　　　　　　　　　　　　　　　　　　　　　　　　　　　　　**07-20/07-29**

Dames　Ladies　Damen　Donne

Fleuret, épr. individuelle　Foil individual　Florett-Einzel　Fioretto individuale

1	Ildiko Schwarczenberger	HUN	4	B*	21/15	4	Brigitte Dumont	FRA	2		17/17
2	Maria Consolata Collino	ITA	4	B*	24/12	5	Cornelia Hanisch	GER	1		13/22
3	Elena Belova	URS	3		21/19	6	Ildiko Bobis	HUN	1		13/24
26	Chantal Payer	CAN									

B—victoire par barrage, victory by barrage

Fleuret, épr. par équipe　Foil team　Florett-Mannschaft　Fioretto a squadra

1	Elena Belova/Olga Kniazeva/Valentina Sidorova/Nailia Guiliazova	URS	52/26
2	Brigitte Latrille/Brigitte Dumont/Christi Muzio/Veroniq Trinquet	FRA	26/52
3	Ildiko Schwarczenberger/Edit Kovacs/Magda Maros/Ildiko Rejtö	HUN	53/39
4	Karin Rutz/Cornelia Hanisch/Ute Kircheis/Brigitte Oertel	GER	39/53
5	Maria C. Collino/Giulia Lorenzoni/Doriana Pigliapoco/Susanna Batazzi	ITA	64/63
6	Jolanta Bebel/Barbara Wysoczanska/Kamilla Skladanowska/Krystyna Machnicka-Urbans	POL	63/64
9	Susan Stewart/Donna Hennyey/Chantal Payer/Fleurette Campeau	CAN	

Messieurs　Men　Herren　Uomini

Epée, épr. individuelle　Epee individual　Degen-Einzel　Spada individuale

1	Alexander Pusch	GER	3	B	22/18
2	Jürgen Hehn	GER	3	B	18/20
3	Gyözö Kulcsar	HUN	3	B	22/19
4	Istvan Ösztrics	HUN	2		18/19
5	Jerzy Janikowski	POL	2		20/21
6	Rolf Edling	SWE	2		18/21
51	Alain Dansereau	CAN			

Fleuret, épr. individuelle　Foil individual　Florett-Einzel　Fioretto individuale

1	Fabio Dal Zotto	ITA	4	B	24/15
2	Alexandr Romankov	URS	4	B	21/13
3	Bernard Talvard	FRA	3		19/21
4	Vassili Stankovich	URS	2		19/18
5	Frédéric Pietruska	FRA	2		13/19
6	Gregory Benko	AUS	0		15/25
41	Michel Dessureault	CAN			

Sabre, épr. individuelle　Sabre individual　Säbel-Einzel　Sciabola individuale

1	Viktor Krovopouskov	URS	5	25/14	4	Ioan Pop	ROM	2	19/20
2	Vladimir Nazlymov	URS	4	23/18	5	Mario A. Montano	ITA	1	16/21
3	Viktor Sidiak	URS	3	22/20	6	Michele Maffei	ITA	0	13/25
30	Marc Lavoie	CAN							

Epée, épr. par équipe   Epee team   Degen-Mannschaft   Spada a squadra

1	Carl von Essen/Hans Jacobson/Rolf Edling/Leif Hogstrom	SWE	64/59
2	Alexander Pusch/Jürgen Hehn/Reinhold Behr/Volker Fischer	GER	59/64
3	Francois Suchanecki/Michel Poffet/Daniel Giger/Christian Kauter	SUI	57/43
4	Istvan Ösztrics/Sandor Erdos/Csaba Fenyvesi/Gyözö Kulcsar	HUN	43/57
5	Alexandr Aboushahmetov/Boris Loukomski/Alexandr Bykov/Viktor Modzolevskiy	URS	54/31
6	Nicolae Iorgu/Paul Szabo/Ioan Popa/Anton Pongratz	ROM	31/54
11	Alain Dansereau/Michel Dessureault/Geza Tatrallyay/George Varaljay	CAN	

Fleuret, épr. par équipe   Foil team   Florett-Mannschaft   Fioretto a squadra

1	Matthias Behr/Thomas Bach/Harald Hein/Klaus Reichert	GER	64/57
2	Fabio Dal Zotto/Carlo Montano/Stefano Simoncelli/Battista Colletti	ITA	57/64
3	Christian Noël/Bernard Talvard/Didier Flament/Frédéric Pietruska	FRA	55/36
4	Vassili Stankovich/Alexandr Romankov/Vladimir Denisov/Sabirjan Rouziev	URS	36/55
5	Ziemowit Wojciechowski/Lech Koziejowski/Leszek Martewicz/Arkadius Godel	POL	48/24
6	Nichloas Bell/Barry Paul/Robert Bruniges/Graham Paul	GBR	24/48

Sabre, épr. par équipe   Sabre team   Säbel-Mannschaft   Sciabola a squadra

1	Viktor Krovopouskov/Edouard Vinokurov/Viktor Sidiak/Vladimir Nazlymov	URS	59/44
2	Mario A. Montano/Michele Maffei/Angelo Arcidiacono/Tommaso Montano	ITA	44/59
3	Dan Irimiciuc/Ioan Pop/Marin Mustata/Cornel Marin	ROM	55/36
4	Peter Marot/Tamas Kovacs/Imre Gedovari/Ferenc Hammang	HUN	36/55
5	Manuel Ortiz/Francisco de Latorre/Guzman Salazar/Ramon Hernandez	CUB	66/56
6	Leszek Jablonowski/Sylweste Krolikowski/Jacek Bierkowski/Josef Nowara	POL	56/66
9	Marc Lavoie/Peter Urban/Imre Nagy/Eli Sukunda	CAN	

Gymnastique/Gymnastics/Turnen/Ginnastica

1976   07-18/07-23

Dames   Ladies   Damen   Donne

Barres asymétriques   Uneven bars   Stufenbarren   Parallele asimmetriche

1	Nadia Comaneci	ROM	10.000	10.00	20.000
2	Teodora Ungureanu	ROM	9.900	9.90	19.800
3	Marta Egervari	HUN	9.875	9.90	19.775
4	Marion Kische	GDR	9.900	9.85	19.750
5	Olga Korbut	URS	9.900	9.40	19.300
6	Nelli Kim	URS	9.825	9.40	19.225
—	Kelly Muncey	CAN	9.475		

Exercices au sol   Floor exercises   Boden   Corpo libero

1	Nelli Kim	URS	9.850	10.00	19.850
2	Ludmila Tourischeva	URS	9.925	9.90	19.825
3	Nadia Comaneci	ROM	9.800	9.95	19.750
4	Anna Pohludkova	TCH	9.725	9.85	19.575
5	Marion Kische	GDR	9.675	9.80	19.475
6	Gitta Escher	GDR	9.700	9.75	19.450
—	Lise Arsenault	CAN	9.375		

Poutre   Balance beam   Schwebebalken   Trave

1	Nadia Comaneci	ROM	9.950	10.00	19.950
2	Olga Korbut	URS	9.825	9.90	19.725
3	Teodora Ungureanu	ROM	9.800	9.90	19.700
4	Ludmila Tourischeva	URS	9.625	9.85	19.475
5	Angelika Hellmann	GDR	9.550	9.90	19.450
6	Gitta Escher	GDR	9.575	9.70	19.275
—	Patti Rope	CAN	9.225		

Saut de cheval   Horse vault   Pferdsprung   Salto del cavallo

1	Nelli Kim	URS	9.850	9.95	19.800
2	Ludmila Tourischeva	URS	9.800	9.85	19.650
	Carola Dombeck	GDR	9.750	9.90	19.650
4	Nadia Comaneci	ROM	9.775	9.85	19.625
5	Gitta Escher	GDR	9.750	9.80	19.550
6	Marta Egervari	HUN	9.700	9.75	19.450
—	Nancy McDonnell	CAN	9.350		

Concours multiple individuel   All-round competition individual   Achtkampf Einzelwertung   Concorso completo individuale

			Saut d. chev / Horse vault / Pferdsprung / Salto d. cav.	Barres asym. / Uneven bars / Stufenbarren / Parall. asim.	Poutre / Beam / Schwebeb. / Trave	Sol / Floor / Boden / Corpo l.		
1	Nadia Comaneci	ROM	39.525	9.85	10.00	10.00	9.90	39.75	79.275
2	Nelli Kim	URS	39.125	10.00	9.90	9.70	9.95	39.55	78.675
3	Ludmila Tourischeva	URS	39.125	9.95	9.80	9.85	9.90	39.50	78.625
4	Teodora Ungureanu	ROM	39.025	9.75	9.90	9.90	9.80	39.35	78.375
5	Olga Korbut	URS	38.975	9.80	9.90	9.50	9.85	39.05	78.025
6	Gitta Escher	GDR	38.800	9.90	9.85	9.55	9.65	38.95	77.750
27	Karen Kelsall	CAN	37.175	9.00	9.60	9.25	9.60	37.45	74.625

			Saut d.chev. Horse vault Pferdsprung Salto d.cav.	Barres asym. Uneven bars Stufenbarren Parall.asim.	Poutre Beam Schwebeb. Trave	Sol Floor Boden Corpo l.	
1	S. Grozdova/E. Saadi M. Filatova/O. Korbut/ L. Tourischeva/N. Kim	URS *imposé/compulsary* *volonté/optional*	48.70 49.00	48.85 49.00	47.95 48.95	48.70 49.20	390.35
2	G. Gabor/A. Grigoras/ M. Constantin/G. Trusca/ T. Ungureanu/N. Comaneci	ROM	47.95 48.05	49.15 49.35	48.05 48.80	47.55 48.25	387.15
3	A. Hellmann/M. Kische/ K. Gerschau/St. Kraker/ G. Escher/C. Dombeck	GDR	47.95 48.75	48.70 49.10	47.10 47.30	47.85 48.35	385.10
4	M. Kelemen/E. Ovari/ K. Medveczky/M. Toth/ M. Lovei/M. Egervari	HUN	47.55 47.95	48.25 48.35	46.20 47.50	46.65 47.70	380.15
5	D. Smolikova/A. Cernakova/ A. Pohludkova/E. Poradkova/ I. Holkovicova/J. Knopova	TCH	46.80 47.30	46.65 48.45	46.45 46.80	47.45 48.35	378.25
6	C. Englert/D. Howard/ K. Chace/L. Wolfsberger/ D. Willcox/C. Casey	USA	47.15 46.85	47.60 48.10	46.05 44.60	46.85 47.85	375.05
9	L. Arsenault/T. McDonnell/ K. Kelsall/K. Muncey/ P. Rope/N. McDonnell	CAN	45.90 46.80	45.75 47.75	44.70 45.30	46.10 47.35	369.65

Gymnastique/Gymnastics/Turnen/Ginnastica

Messieurs   Men   Herren   Uomini

Anneaux   Rings   Ringe   Anelli

1	Nikolai Andrianov	URS	9.850	9.80	19.650
2	Alexandr Ditiation	URS	9.750	9.80	19.550
3	Danut Grecu	ROM	9.750	9.75	19.500
4	Ferenc Donath	HUN	9.650	9.55	19.200
5	Eizo Kemmotsu	JPN	9.625	9.55	19.175
6	Sawao Kato	JPN	9.625	9.50	19.125
—	Pierre Leclerc	CAN	9.225		

Barre fixe   Horizontal bar   Reck   Sbarra

1	Mitsuo Tsukahara	JPN	9.825	9.85	19.675
2	Eizo Kemmotsu	JPN	9.750	9.75	19.500
3	Eberhard Gienger	GER	9.675	9.80	19.475
	Henri Boerio	FRA	9.675	9.80	19.475
5	Gennadi Kryssin	URS	9.650	9.60	19.250
6	Ferenc Donath	HUN	9.600	9.60	19.200
—	Philip Delesalle	CAN	9.325		

Barres parallèles   Parallel bars   Barren   Parallele

1	Sawao Kato	JPN	9.775	9.90	19.675
2	Nikolai Andrianov	URS	9.750	9.75	19.500
3	Mitsuo Tsukahara	JPN	9.675	9.80	19.475
4	Bernd Jäger	GDR	9.600	9.60	19.200
5	Miloslav Netusil	TCH	9.525	9.60	19.125
6	Andrzej Szajna	POL	9.500	9.45	18.950
—	Pierre Leclerc	CAN	9.300		

Cheval d'arçon   Side horse   Seitpferd   Cavallo con Maniglie

1	Zoltan Magyar	HUN	9.800	9.90	19.700
2	Eizo Kemmotsu	JPN	9.775	9.80	19.575
3	Nikolai Andrianov	URS	9.725	9.80	19.525
	Michael Nikolay	GDR	9.725	9.80	19.525
5	Sawao Kato	JPN	9.700	9.70	19.400
6	Alexandr Ditiatin	URS	9.650	9.70	19.350
—	Keith Carter	CAN	8.925		

Exercices au sol   Floor exercises   Boden   Corpo libero

1	Nikolai Andrianov	URS	9.650	9.80	19.450
2	Vladimir Marchenko	URS	9.675	9.75	19.425
3	Peter Kormann	USA	9.500	9.80	19.300
4	Roland Bruckner	GDR	9.525	9.75	19.275
5	Sawao Kato	JPN	9.600	9.65	19.250
6	Eizo Kemmotsu	JPN	9.550	9.55	19.100
—	Keith Carter	CAN	9.175		

Saut cheval   Horse vault   Pferdsprung   Salto al Cavallo

1	Nikolai Andrianov	URS	9.675	9.775	19.450
2	Mitsuo Tsukahara	JPN	9.650	9.725	19.375
3	Hiroshi Kajiyama	JPN	9.675	9.600	19.275
4	Danut Grecu	ROM	9.650	9.550	19.200
5	Zoltan Magyar	HUN	9.575	9.575	19.150
	Imre Molnar	HUN	9.725	9.425	19.150
—	Keith Carter	CAN	9.375		

Concours multiple individuel		All-round competition individual		Zwölfkampf Einzelwertung		Concorso completo individuale				
				Sol Floor Boden Corpol.	Chev. d'arcon Side horse Seitpferd Cav. maniglie	Anneaux Rings Ringe Anelli	Saut d. chev Horse vault Pferdsprung Salto d. cav.	Barres par. Par. bars Barren Parallele	Barre Fixe Horiz. bar Reck Sbarra	
1	Nikolai Andrianov	URS	58.250	9.80	9.70	9.75	9.80	9.65	9.70	58.40	116.650
2	Sawao Kato	JPN	57.950	9.60	9.60	9.45	9.55	9.70	9.80	57.70	115.650
3	Mitsuo Tsukahara	JPN	57.875	9.50	9.60	9.40	9.80	9.70	9.70	57.70	115.575
4	Alexandr Ditiatin	URS	57.575	9.70	9.70	9.75	9.75	9.60	9.45	57.95	115.525
5	Hiroshi Kajiyama	JPN	57.625	9.60	9.65	9.65	9.65	9.65	9.60	57.80	115.425
6	Andrzej Szajna	POL	56.925	9.60	9.60	9.60	9.80	9.55	9.55	57.70	114.625
22	Philip Delesalle	CAN	54.500	9.30	9.65	9.35	9.50	9.30	9.15	56.25	110.750

Concours par équipes		All-round competition Team		Zwölfkampf Mannschaft		Concorso multiplo				
				Sol Floor Boden Corpol.	Chev. d'arcon Side horse Seitpferd Cav. maniglie	Anneaux Rings Ringe Anelli	Saut d. chev Horse vault Pferdsprung Salto d. cav.	Barres par. Par. bars Barren Parallele	Barre Fixe Horiz. bar Reck Sbarra	
1	H. Igarashi/S. Fujimoto/ H. Kajiyama/M. Tsukahara/ E. Kemmotsu/S. Kato	JPN	imposé/compulsory volonte/optional	47.20 47.95	47.70 48.70	47.20 48.65	47.80 47.85	48.15 48.30	48.25 49.10	576.85
2	V. Tikhonov/G. Kryssin/ V. Marchenko/A. Ditiatión/ V. Markelov/N. Andrianov	URS		47.80 48.80	48.00 47.90	48.00 49.35	47.60 47.60	47.70 47.60	47.70 48.40	576.45
3	B. Jäger/M. Nikolay/ R. Hanschke/L. Mack/ W. Klotz/R. Bruckner	GDR		46.50 47.25	47.20 47.40	46.55 47.80	46.85 46.85	47.00 46.65	47.15 47.45	564.65
4	A. Farkas/I. Banrevi/ B. Laufer/F. Donath/ I. Molnar/Z. Magyar	HUN		45.40 47.00	46.75 47.50	46.75 47.80	47.85 47.85	47.00 46.10	46.90 47.55	564.45
5	R. Dietze/R. Ritter/ W. Steinmetz/V. Rohrwick/ E. Jorek/E. Gienger	GER		45.95 46.70	45.85 46.90	45.85 47.85	46.65 46.70	45.30 46.10	46.50 47.05	557.40
6	S. Gal/M. Bors/ S. Cepoi/N. Oprescu/ D. Grecu/I. Checiches	ROM		44.90 45.45	45.10 46.40	46.90 48.30	46.90 47.45	46.85 46.15	45.85 47.05	557.30

Haltérophilie/Weightlifting/Gewichtheben/Sollevamento pesi

1976   07-18/07-28

–52 kg Poids mouche Flyweight Fliegengewicht Mosca			Arraché Snatch Reissen Strappo	Epaulé & jeté Clean & jerk Stossen Spinta		
1	Alexandr Voronin	URS	105.0	137.5	RO/OR	242.5
2	György Koszegi	HUN	107.5	130.0		237.5
3	Mohammad Nassiri- Seresht	IRN	100.0	135.0		235.0
4	Masatomo Takeuchi	JPN	105.0	127.5		232.5
5	Francisco Casamayor	CUB	100.0	127.5		227.5
6	Stefan Leletko	POL	95.0	125.0		220.0

–56 kg Poids coq Bantamweight Bantamgewicht Gallo			Arraché Snatch Reissen Strappo	Epaulé & jeté Clean & jerk Stossen Spinta		
1	Norair Nurikyan	BUL	117.5	145.0	RM/WR	262.5
2	Grzegorz Cziura	POL	115.0	137.5		252.5
3	Kenkichi Ando	JPN	107.5	142.5		250.0
4	Leszek Skorupa	POL	112.5	137.5		250.0
5	Imre Földi	HUN	105.0	140.0		245.0
6	Bernhard Bachfisch	GER	105.0	137.5		242.5
—	Yves Carignan	CAN				Elimin.

–60 kg Poids plume Featherweight Federgewicht Piuma			Arraché Snatch Reissen Strappo	Epaulé & jeté Clean & jerk Stossen Spinta		
1	Nikolai Kolesnikov	URS	125.0	160.0	RO/OR	285.0
2	Georgi Todorov	BUL	122.5	157.5		280.0
3	Kazumasa Hirai	JPN	125.0	150.0		275.0
4	Takashi Saito	JPN	110.0	152.5		262.5
5	Edward Weitz	ISR	110.0	152.5		262.5
6	Davoud Maleki	IRN	115.0	145.0		260.0

–67.5 kg Poids léger Lightweight Leichtgewicht Leggeri			Arraché Snatch Reissen Strappo	Epaulé & jeté Clean & jerk Stossen Spinta		
1	Zbigniew Kaczmarek*	POL	135.0	172.5	RO/OR	307.5
2	Piotr Korol	URS	135.0	170.0		305.0
3	Daniel Senet	FRA	135.0	165.0		300.0
4	Kazimierz Czarnecki	POL	130.0	165.0		295.0
5	Günter Ambrass	GDR	125.0	170.0		295.0
6	Yatsuo Shimaya	JPN	127.5	165.0		292.5

−75 kg

	Poids moyen Middleweight Mittelgewicht Medi		Arraché Snatch Reissen Strappo	Epaulé & jeté Clean & jerk Stossen Spinta		
1	Yordan Mitkov	BUL	145.0	190.0	**RO/OR**	335.0
2	Vartan Militosyan	URS	145.0	185.0		330.0
3	Peter Wenzel	GDR	145.0	182.5		327.5
4	Wolfgang Hübner	GDR	142.5	177.5		320.0
5	Arvo Ala-Pontio	FIN	137.5	177.5		315.0
6	Andras Stark	HUN	140.0	175.0		315.0

−82.5 kg

	Poids mi-lourd Light heavyweight Leichtschwergewicht Massimi leggeri		Arraché Snatch Reissen Strappo	Epaulé & jeté Clean & jerk Stossen Spinta		
1	Valeri Shary	URS	162.5	202.5	**RO/OR**	365.0
2	Blagoi Blagoev*	BUL	162.5	200.0		362.5
3	Trendafil Stoichev	BUL	162.5	197.5		360.0
4	Peter Baczako	HUN	157.5	187.5		345.0
5	Nicolaos Iliadis	GRE	150.0	190.0		340.0
6	Juhani Avellan	FIN	145.0	185.0		330.0
—	Pierre St-Jean	CAN				*Elimin.*

−90 kg

	Poids lourd-léger Middle heavyweight Mittelschwergewicht Massimi medio		Arraché Snatch Reissen Strappo	Epaulé & jeté Clean & jerk Stossen Spinta		
1	David Rigert	URS	170.0	212.5	**RO/OR**	382.0
2	Lee James	USA	165.0	197.5		362.5
3	Atanas Shopov	BUL	155.0	205.0		360.0
4	Philip Grippaldi	USA	150.0	205.0		355.0
5	György Rehus-Uzor	HUN	157.5	192.5		350.0
6	Peter Petzold	GDR	152.5	192.5		345.0

−110 kg

	Poids lourd Heavyweight Schwergewicht Massimi		Arraché Snatch Reissen Strappo	Epaulé & jeté Clean & jerk Stossen Spinta		
1	Valentin Christov*	BUL	175.0	225.0	**RO/OR**	400.0
2	Yuri Zaitsev	URS	165.0	220.0		385.0
3	Krastio Semerdjiev	BUL	170.0	215.0		385.0
4	Tadeusz Rutkowski	POL	167.5	210.0		377.5
5	Mark Cameron*	USA	162.5	212.5		375.0
6	Pierre Gourrier	FRA	157.5	215.0		372.5
11	Russ Prior	CAN	167.5	195.0		362.5

+ 110 kg

	Poids super-lourd Super heavyweight Super Schwergewicht Super massimo		Arraché Snatch Reissen Strappo	Epaulé & jeté Clean & jerk Stossen Spinta		
1	Vasili Alexeev	URS	185.0	255.0	**RO/OR**	440.0
2	Gerd Bonk	GDR	170.0	235.0		405.0
3	Helmut Losch	GDR	165.0	222.5		387.5
4	Jan Nagy	TCH	160.0	227.5		387.5
5	Bruce Wilhelm	USA	172.5	215.0		387.5
6	Petr Pavlasek	TCH	172.5	215.0		387.5

Déclassements possibles après les contrôles anti-dopants.

Possible disqualifications following anti-doping controls.

Judo

−63 kg

Poids léger
Lightweight
Leichtgewicht
Leggeri

1	Hector Rodriguez	CUB
2	Eunkyung Chang	KOR
3	Jozsef Tuncsik	HUN
	Felice Mariani	ITA
—	Brad Farrow	CAN*

−70 kg

Poids mi-moyen
Light Middleweight
Weltergewicht
Welter

1	Vladimir Nevzorov	URS
2	Koji Kuramoto	JPN
3	Patrick Vial	FRA
	Marian Talaj	POL

−80 kg

Poids moyen
Middleweight
Mittelgewicht
Medio

1	Isamu Sonoda	JPN
2	Valery Dvoinikov	URS
3	Slavko Obadov	YUG
	Youngchul Park	KOR
—	Rainer Fischer	CAN*

−93 kg

Poids mi-lourd
Light heavyweight
Halbschwergewicht
Medio massimi

1	Kazuhiro Ninomiya	JPN
2	Ramaz Harshiladze	URS
3	David Starbrook	GBR
	Jürg Roethlisberger	SUI
—	Joe Meli	CAN*

−93 kg

Poids lourd
Heavyweight
Schwergewicht
Massimo

1	Sergei Novikov	URS
2	Güenther Neureuther	GER
3	Allen Coage	USA
	Sumio Endo	JPN

Toutes catégories

Open category
Offene Klasse
Aperta

1	Haruki Uemura	JPN
2	Keith Remfry	GBR
3	Shota Chochishvilli	URS
	Jeaki Cho	KOR
—	Tom Greenway	CAN*

Lutte/Wrestling/Ringen/Lotta

Libre   Free Style   Freistil   Libera

–48 kg		
Poids mi-mouche		
Light flyweight		
Papiergewicht		
Mosca leggeri		
1	Khassan Issaev	BUL
2	Roman Dmitriev	URS
3	Akira Kudo	JPN
4	Gombo Khishigbaatar	MGL
5	Hwa-Kyung Kim	KOR
6	Yong Nam Li	PRK
—	Ray Takahashi	CAN*

–52 kg		
Poids mouche		
Flyweight		
Fliegengewicht		
Mosca		
1	Yuji Takada	JPN
2	Alexandr Ivanov	URS
3	Hae-Sup Jeon	KOR
4	Henrik Gal	HUN
5	Nermedin Selimov	BUL
6	Wladysla Stecyk	POL
—	Bertie Gordon	CAN*

–57 kg		
Poids coq		
Bantamweight		
Bantamgewicht		
Gallo		
1	Vladimir Umin	URS
2	Hans-Dieter Bruchert	GDR
3	Masao Arai	JPN
4	Mikho Doukov	BUL
5	Ramezan Kheder	IRN
6	Migd Khoilogdorj	MGL
—	Michael Barry	CAN*

–62 kg		
Poids plume		
Featherweight		
Federgewicht		
Piuma		
1	Jung-Mo Yang	KOR
2	Zeveg Oidov	MGL
3	Gene Davis	USA
4	M. Farahvashi-Fashandi	IRN
5	Ivan Yankov	BUL
6	Sergey Timofeev	URS
—	Egon Beiler	CAN*

–68 kg		
Poids léger		
Lightweight		
Leichtgewicht		
Leggeri		
1	Pavel Pinigin	URS
2	Lloyd Keaser	USA
3	Yasaburo Sugawara	JPN
4	Dontcho Jekov	BUL
5	Jose Ramos	CUB
6	Tsedendamba Natsagdorj	MGL
—	Clive Llewellyn	CAN*

–74 kg		
Poids mi-moyen		
Welterweight		
Weltergewicht		
Welter		
1	Jiichiro Date	JPN
2	Mansour Barzegar	IRN
3	Stanley Dziedzic	USA
4	Ruslan Ashuraliev	URS
5	Marin Pircalabu	ROM
6	Fred Hempel	GDR
—	Brian Renken	CAN*

–82 kg		
Poids moyen		
Middleweight		
Mittelgewicht		
Medi		
1	John Peterson	USA
2	Viktor Novojilov	URS
3	Adolf Seger	GER
4	Mehmet Uzun	TUR
5	Ismail Abilov	BUL
6	Henryk Mazur	POL
—	Richard Deschatelets	CAN*

–90 kg		
Poids mi-lourd		
Light heavyweight		
Halbschwergewicht		
Medio massimo		
1	Levan Tediashvili	URS
2	Benjamin Peterson	USA
3	Stelica Morcov	ROM
4	Horst Stottmeister	GDR
5	Terry Paice	CAN
6	Pawel Kurczewski	POL
—	Terry Paice	CAN*

–100 kg		
Poids lourd		
Heavyweight		
Schwergewicht		
Massimo		
1	Ivan Yarygin	URS
2	Russell Hellickson	USA
3	Dimo Kostov	BUL
4	Petr Drozda	TCH
5	Khorloo Baianmunkh	MGL
6	Kazuo Shimizu	JPN
—	Steve Daniar	CAN*

+ 100 kg								
Poids super-lourd								
Super heavyweight								
Super Schwergewicht								
Super massimo								
1	Soslan Andiev	URS	4	Roland Gehrke	GDR	—	Harry Geris	CAN*
2	Jozsef Balla	HUN	5	Nikola Dinev	BUL			
3	Ladislau Simon	ROM	6	Yorihide Isogai	JPN			*elimin.*

Greco-romaine   Greco-roman   Griechisch-Römisch   Greco-romana

–48 kg		
Poids mi-mouche		
Light flyweight		
Papiergewicht		
Mosca leggeri		
1	Alexey Shumakov	URS
2	Gheorghe Berceanu	ROM
3	Stefan Anghelov	BUL
4	Yoshite Moriwaki	JPN
5	Dietmar Hinz	GDR
6	Mitchell Kawasaki	CAN

–52 kg		
Poids mouche		
Flyweight		
Fliegengewicht		
Mosca		
1	Vitaly Konstantinov	URS
2	Nicu Ginga	ROM
3	Koichiro Hirayama	JPN
4	Rolf Krauss	GER
5	Lajos Racz	HUN
6	Morad-Ali Shirani	IRN

–57 kg		
Poids coq		
Bantamweight		
Bantamgewicht		
Gallo		
1	Pertti Ukkola	FIN
2	Ivan Frgic	YUG
3	Farhat Mustafin	URS
4	Yoshima Suga	JPN
5	Mihai Botila	ROM
6	Krasimir Stefanov	BUL
—	Doug Yeats	CAN*

–62 kg
Poids plume
Featherweight
Federgewicht
Piuma

1	Kazimier Lipien	POL
2	Nelson Davidian	URS
3	Laszlo Reczi	HUN
4	Teruhiko Miyahara	JPN
5	Ion Paun	ROM
6	Pekka Hjelt	FIN
—	Howard Stupp	CAN*

–68 kg
Poids léger
Lightweight
Leichtgewicht
Leggeri

1	Suren Nalbandyan	URS
2	Stefan Rusu	ROM
3	Heinz-Helmut Wehling	GDR
4	Lars Skiold	SWE
5	Andrzej Supron	POL
6	Manfred Schondorfer	GER
—	John McPhedran	CAN*

–74 kg
Poids mi-moyen
Welterweight
Weltergewicht
Welter

1	Anatolyi Bykov	URS
2	Vitezslav Macha	TCH
3	Karl-Heinz Helbig	GER
4	Mikko Huhtala	FIN
5	Klaus-Dieter Göpfert	GDR
6	Gheorghe Ciobotaru	ROM
—	Brian Renken	CAN*

–82 kg
Poids moyen
Middleweight
Mittelgewicht
Medi

1	Momir Petkovic	YUG
2	Vladimir Cheboksarov	URS
3	Ivan Kolev	BUL
4	Leif Andersson	SWE
5	Miroslav Janota	TCH
6	Kazuhiro Takanishi	JPN
—	David Cummings	CAN*

–90 kg
Poids mi-lourd
Light heavyweight
Halbschwergewicht
Medio massimo

1	Valery Rezantsev	URS
2	Stoyan Ivanov	BUL
3	Czeslaw Kwiecinski	POL
4	Darko Nisavic	YUG
5	Frank Andersson	SWE
6	Istvan Sellyei	HUN

–100 kg
Poids lourd
Heavyweight
Schwergewicht
Massimo

1	Nikolai Bolboshin	URS
2	Kamen Goranov	BUL
3	Andrzej Skrzylewski	POL
4	Brad Rheingans	USA
5	Tore Hem	NOR
6	Heinz Schäfer	GER

+ 100 kg
Poids super-lourd
Super heavyweight
Super Schwergewicht
Super massimo

1	Alexandr Kolchinski	URS	4	Henryk Tomanek	POL	
2	Alexandr Tomov	BUL	5	William Lee	USA	
3	Roman Codreanu	ROM	6	Janos Rovnyai	HUN	

*elimin.

Natation/Swimming/Schwimmen/Nuoto

1976	07-18/07-27

Dames   Ladies   Damen   Donne

100 m   Brasse   Breaststroke   Brust   Rana

1	Hannelore Anke	GDR		1:11.16
2	Liubov Rusanova	URS		1:13.04
3	Marina Koshevaia	URS		1:13.30
4	Carola Nitschke	GDR		1:13.33
5	Gabriele Askamp	GER		1:14.15
6	Marina Iurchenia	URS		1:14.17
9	Robin Corsiglia	CAN		1:14.56

200 m   Brasse   Breaststroke   Brust   Rana

1	Marina Koshevaia	URS	RO/OR	2:33.35
2	Marina Iurchenia	URS		2:36.08
3	Liubov Rusanova	URS		2:36.22
4	Hannelore Anke	GDR		2:36.49
5	Karla Linke	GDR		2:36.97
6	Carola Nitschke	GDR		2:38.27
9	Joann Baker	CAN		2:39.27

100 m   Dos   Backstroke   Rücken   Dorso

1	Ulrike Richter	GDR	RO/OR	1:01.83
2	Birgit Treiber	GDR		1:03.41
3	Nancy Garapick	CAN		1:03.71
4	Wendy Hogg	CAN		1:03.93
5	Cheryl Gibson	CAN		1:05.16
6	Nadejda Stavko	URS		1:05.19

200 m   Dos   Backstroke   Rücken   Dorso

1	Ulrike Richter	GDR	RO/OR	2:13.43
2	Birgit Treiber	GDR		2:14.97
3	Nancy Garapick	CAN		2:15.60
4	Nadejda Stavko	URS		2:16.28
5	Melissa Belote	USA		2:17.27
6	Antje Stille	GDR		2:17.55

100 m   Nage libre   Freestyle   Kraul   Stile libero

1	Kornelia Ender	GDR	RM/WR	55.65
2	Petra Priemer	GDR		56.49
3	Enith Brigitha	HOL		56.65
4	Kim Peyton	USA		56.81
5	Shirley Babashoff	USA		56.95
6	Claudia Hempel	GDR		56.99
9	Barbara Clark	CAN		57.72

200 m   Nage libre   Freestyle   Kraul   Stile libero

1	Kornelia Ender	GDR	RM/WR	1:59.26
2	Shirley Babashoff	USA		2:01.22
3	Enith Brigitha	HOL		2:01.40
4	Annelies Maas	HOL		2:02.56
5	Gail Amundrud	CAN		2:03.32
6	Jennifer Hooker	USA		2:04.20
13	Debbie Clarke	CAN		2:05.10

400 m	Nage libre	Freestyle	Kraul	Stile libero		
1	Petra Thümer		GDR	RM/WR	4:09.89
2	Shirley Babashoff		USA		4:10.46
3	Shannon Smith		CAN		4:14.60
4	Rebecca Perrott		NZL		4:14.76
5	Kathy Heddy		USA		4:15.50
6	Brenda Borgh		USA		4:17.43

800 m	Nage libre	Freestyle	Kraul	Stile libero		
1	Petra Thümer		GDR	RM/WR	8:37.14
2	Shirley Babashoff		USA		8:37.59
3	Wendy Weinberg		USA		8:42.60
4	Rosemary Milgate		AUS		8:47.21
5	Nicole Kramer		USA		8:47.33
6	Shannon Smith		CAN		8:48.15

100 m	Papillon	Butterfly	Delphin	Delfino		
1	Kornelia Ender		GDR	RM/WR	1:00.13
2	Andrea Pollack		GDR		1:00.98
3	Wendy Boglioli		USA		1:01.17
4	Camille Wright		USA		1:01.41
5	Rosemarie Gabriel		GDR		1:01.56
6	Wendy Quirk		CAN		1:01.75

200 m	Papillon	Butterfly	Delphin	Delfino		
1	Andrea Pollack		GDR	RO/OR	2:11.41
2	Ulrike Tauber		GDR		2:12.50
3	Rosemarie Gabriel		GDR		2:12.86
4	Karen Thornton		USA		2:12.90
5	Wendy Quirk		CAN		2:13.68
6	Cheryl Gibson		CAN		2:13.91

400 m	Quatre nages	Individual medley	Lagen	Quattro stili		
1	Ulrike Tauber		GDR	RM/WR	4:42.77
2	Cheryl Gibson		CAN		4:48.10
3	Beckey Smith		CAN		4:50.48
4	Birgit Treiber		GDR		4:52.40
5	Sabine Kahle		GDR		4:53.50
6	Donnalee Wennerstrom		USA		4:55.34

4 x 100 m	Relais nage libre	Freestyle relay	Kraulstaffel	Staffeta stile libero		
1	Kim Peyton/Wendy Boglioli/Jill Sterkel/Shirley Babashoff			USA	RM/WR	3.44.82
2	Kornelia Ender/Petra Priemer/Andrea Pollack/Claudia Hempel			GDR		3:45.50
3	Gail Amundrud, Barbara Clark/Becky Smith/Anne Jardin			CAN		3:48.81
4	Ineke Ran/Linda Faber/Annelies Maas/Enith Brigitha			HOL		3:51.67
5	Liubov Kobzova/Irina Vlasova/Marina Kliuchnikova/Larisa Tsareva			URS		3:52.69
6	Guylaine Berger/Sylvie le Noach/Caroline Carpentier/Chantal Schertz			FRA		3:56.73

4 x 100 m	Relais quatre nages	Medley relay	Lagenstaffel	Staffetta mista		
1	Ulrike Richter/Hannelore Anke/Andrea Pollack/Kornelia Ender			GDR	RM/WR	4:07.95
2	Linde Jezek/Lauri Siering/Camille Wright/Shirley Babashoff			USA		4:14.55
3	Wendy Hogg/Robin Corsiglia/Susan Sloan/Anne Jardin			CAN		4:15.22
4	Nadejda Stavko/Marina Iurchenia/Tamara Shelofastova/Larisa Tsareva			URS		4:16.05
5	Diane Edelijn/Wyda Mazereeuw/Jose Damen/Enith Brigitha			HOL		4:19.93
6	Joy Beasley/Margaret Kelly/Susan Jenner/Deborah Hill			GBR		4:23.25

Plongeon du tremplin	Springboard diving			
Kunstspringen	Tuffo trampolino			
1	Jennifer Chandler		USA	506.19
2	Christa Köhler		GDR	469.41
3	Cynthia McIngvale		USA	466.83
4	Heidi Ramlow		GDR	462.15
5	Karin Guthke		GDR	459.81
6	Olga Dmitrieva		URS	432:24
9	Beverley Boys		CAN	420.57

Plongeon de haut-vol	Platform diving			
Turmspringen	Tuffo piattaforma			
1	Elena Vaytsekhovskaia		URS	406.59
2	Ulrika Knape		SWE	402.60
3	Deborah Wilson		USA	401.07
4	Irina Kalinina		URS	398.67
5	Cindy Shatto		CAN	389.58
6	Teri York		CAN	378.39
14	Tammy Macleod		CAN	332.07

Messieurs   Men   Herren   Uomini

100 m	Brasse	Breaststroke	Brust	Rana		
1	John Hencken		USA	RM/WR	1:03.11
2	David Wilkie		GBR		1:03.43
3	Arvidas Iuozaytis		URS		1:04.23
4	Graham Smith		CAN		1:04.26
5	Giorgio Lalle		ITA		1:04.37
6	Walter Kusch		GER		1:04.38

200 m	Brasse	Breaststroke	Brust	Rana		
1	David Wilkie		GBR	RM/WR	2:15.11
2	John Hencken		USA		2:17.26
3	Rick Colella		USA		2:19.20
4	Graham Smith		CAN		2:19.42
5	Charles Keating		USA		2:20.79
6	Arvidas Iuozaytis		URS		2:21.87

100 m	Dos	Backstroke	Rücken	Dorso		
1	John Naber		USA	RM/WR	55.49
2	Peter Rocca		USA		56.34
3	Roland Matthes		GDR		57.22
4	Carlos Berrocal		PUR		57.28
5	Lutz Wanja		GDR		57.49
6	Bob Jackson		USA		57.69
10	Stephen Pickell		CAN		58.21

200 m	Dos	Backstroke	Rücken	Dorso		
1	John Naber		USA	RM/WR	1:59.19
2	Peter Rocca		USA		2:00.55
3	Dan Harrigan		USA		2:01.35
4	Mark Tonelli		AUS		2:03.17
5	Mark Kerry		AUS		2:04.07
6	Miloslav Rolko		TCH		2:05.81
9	Mike Scarth		CAN		2:07.16

100 m	Nage libre	Freestyle	Kraul	Stile libero		
1	Jim Montgomery		USA		RM/WR	49.99
2	Jack Babashoff		USA			50.81
3	Peter Nocke		GER			51.31
4	Klaus Steinbach		GER			51.68
5	Marcello Guarducci		ITA			51.70
6	Joe Bottom		USA			51.79
11	Stephen Pickell		CAN			52.89

200 m	Nage libre	Freestyle	Kraul	Stile libero		
1	Bruce Furniss		USA		RM/WR	1:50.29
2	John Naber		USA			1:50.50
3	Jim Montgomery		USA			1:50.58
4	Andrey Krylov		URS			1:50.73
5	Klaus Steinbach		GER			1:51.09
6	Peter Nocke		GER			1:51.71
12	Stephen Badger		CAN			1:53.86

400 m	Nage libre	Freestyle	Kraul	Stile libero		
1	Brian Goodell		USA		RM/WR	3:51.93
2	Tim Shaw		USA			3:52.54
3	Vladimir Raskatov		URS			3:55.76
4	Djan G. Madruga		BRA			3:57.18
5	Stephen Holland		AUS			3:57.59
6	Sandor Nagy		HUN			3:57.81
8	Stephen Badger		CAN			4:02.83

1500 m	Nage libre	Freestyle	Kraul	Stile libero		
1	Brian Goodell		USA		RM/WR	15:02.40
2	Bobby Hackett		USA			15:03.91
3	Stephen Holland		AUS			15:04.66
4	Djan G. Madruga		BRA			15:19.84
5	Vladimir Salnikov		URS			15:29.45
6	Max Metzker		AUS			15:31.53
14	Paul Midgley		CAN			15:49.78

100 m	Papillon	Butterfly	Delphin	Delfino		
1	Matt Vogel		USA			54.35
2	Joe Bottom		USA			54.50
3	Gary Hall		USA			54.65
4	Roger Pyttel		GDR			55.09
5	Roland Matthes		GDR			55.11
6	Clay Evans		CAN			55.81
11	Stephen Pickell		CAN			56.66

200 m	Papillon	Butterfly	Delphin	Delfino		
1	Mike Bruner		USA		RM/WR	1:59.23
2	Steven Gregg		USA			1:59.54
3	Bill Forrester		USA			1:59.96
4	Roger Pyttel		GDR			2:00.02
5	Michael Kraus		GER			2:00.46
6	Brian Brinkley		GBR			2:01.49
10	George Nagy		CAN			2:03.33

400 m	Quatre nages	Individual medley	Lagen	Quattro stili		
1	Rod Strachan		USA		RM/WR	4:23.68
2	Tim McKee		USA			4:24.62
3	Andrey Smirnov		URS			4:26.90
4	Andras Hargitay		HUN			4:27.13
5	Graham Smith		CAN			4:28.64
6	Steve Furniss		USA			4:29.23

4 x 200 m	Relais nage libre	Freestyle relay	Kraulstaffel	Staffetta stile libero		
1	Mike Bruner/Bruce Furniss/John Naber/Jim Montgomery			USA	RM/WR	7:23.22
2	Vladimir Raskatov/Andrey Bogdanov/Sergey Kopliakov/Andrey Krylov			URS		7:27.97
3	Alan McClatchey/David Dunne/Gordon Downie/Brian Brinkley			GBR		7:32.11
4	Klaus Steinbach/Peter Nocke/Werner Lampe/Hans-J. Geisler			GER		7:32.27
5	Roger Pyttel/Wilfried Hartung/Rainer Strohbach/Frank Pfutze			GDR		7:38.92
6	Abdul Ressang/Rene van der Kuil/Andre in het Veld/Henk Elzerman			HOL		7:42.56
18	Stephen Badger/Bill Sawchuk/Stephen Pickell/James Hett			CAN		disqualification

400 x 100 m	Relais quatre nages	Medley relay	Lagenstaffel	Staffetta mista		
1	John Naber/John Hencken/Matt Vogel/Jim Montgomery			USA	RM/WR	3:42.22
2	Stephen Pickell/Graham Smith/Clay Evans/Gary Macdonald			CAN		3:45.94
3	Klaus Steinbach/Walter Kusch/Michael Kraus/Peter Nocke			GER		3:47.29
4	James Carter/David Wilkie/John Mills/Brian Brinkley			GBR		3:49.56
5	Igor Omelchenko/Arvidas Iuozaytis/Evgeniy Seredin/Andrey Krylov			URS		3:49.90
6	Mark Kerry/Paul Jarvie/Neil Rogers/Peter Coughlan			AUS		3:51.54

Plongeon du tremplin	Springboard diving	Kunstspringen	Tuffo trampolino	
1	Philip Boggs	USA		619.05
2	Franco Cagnotto	ITA		570.48
3	Aleksandr Kosenkov	URS		567.24
4	Falk Hoffmann	GDR		553.53
5	Robert Cragg	USA		548.19
6	Gregory Louganis	USA		528.96
16	Scott Cranham	CAN		485.97

Plongeon de haut-vol	Platform diving	Turmspringen	Tuffo piattaforma	
1	Klaus Dibiasi	ITA		600.51
2	Gregory Louganis	USA		576.99
3	Vladimir Aleynik	URS		548.61
4	Kent Vosler	USA		544.14
5	Patrick Moore	USA		538.17
6	Falk Hoffmann	GDR		531.60
14	Ken Armstrong	CAN		467.13

Pentathlon moderne/Modern pentathlon/Moderner Fünfkampf/ Pentathlon moderne

Messieurs Men Herren Uomini

Individuel Individual Einzelwertung Individuale

			5 km Equitation Riding Reiten Equitazione	Escrime Fencing Fechten Scherma	Tir Shooting Schiessen Tiro	300 m Natation Swimming Schwimmen Nuoto	4000 m Course à pied Cross country run. Geländelauf Corsa a piedi	
1	Janusz Pyciak-Peciak	POL	1066	928	1044	1164	1318	5520
2	Pavel Lednev	URS	1032	1096	1022	1092	1243	5485
3	Jan Bartu	TCH	1100	976	1044	1184	1162	5466
4	Daniele Masala	ITA	1090	832	1066	1244	1201	5433
5	Adrian Parker	GBR	1100	712	868	1240	1378	5298
6	John Fitzgerald	USA	1036	952	1000	1232	1066	5286
43	John Hawes	CAN	1068	856	230	1272	1108	4534

Equipe Team Mannschaft Squadra

1	Adrian Parker	GBR	1100	752	868	1240	1378	15559
	Robert Nightingale		1012	814	934	1172	1309	
	Jeremy Fox		1100	690	846	1080	1264	
2	Jan Bartu	TCH	1100	969	1044	1184	1162	15451
	Bohumil Starnovsky		1068	876	868	1144	1144	
	Jiri Adam		794	938	1088	1072	1000	
3	Tamas Kancsal	HUN	866	990	956	1164	1219	15395
	Tibor Maracsko		972	845	890	1204	1228	
	Szvetiszlav Sasics		934	938	912	1160	1117	
4	Janusz Pyciak-Peciak	POL	1066	969	1044	1164	1318	15343
	Zbigniew Pacelt		1100	535	890	1308	1138	
	Krzyszto Trybusiewicz		1004	628	978	1072	1129	
5	John Fitzgerald	USA	1036	969	1000	1232	1066	15285
	Michael Burley		1068	752	692	1212	1327	
	Robert Nieman		1036	814	604	1324	1153	
6	Daniele Masala	ITA	1090	907	1066	1244	1201	15031
	Paolo P. Cristofori		1100	721	780	1128	1207	
	Mario Medda		1004	628	824	1056	1075	
13	John D. Hawes	CAN	1068	845	230	1272	1108	12772
	George Skene		1100	504	274	1176	1102	
	Jack Alexander		478	442	692	1268	1213	

Sports equestres/Equestrian sports/Reitsport/Sport equestri

Concours complet par équipe Three day event team Military Mannschaftswertung Concorso completo squadra

			Dressage Dressage Dressur Dressage	Epreuve de fond Endurance test Geländeritt Gara di fondo	Sauts d'obstacles Jumping Springen Salto ad ostacoli	
1	Edmond Coffin (Bally-Cor)	USA	64.59	50.4	0.00	441.00
	John Plumb (Better&Better)		66.25	49.6	10.00	
	Bruce Davidson (Irish-Cap)		54.16	136.0	10.00	
2	Karl Schulz (Madrigal)	GER	46.25	63.2	20.00	584.60
	Herbert Blöcker (Albrant)		108.75	94.4	10.00	
	Helmut Rethemeier (Pauline)		70.00	152.0	20.00	
3	Wayne Roycroft (Laurenson)	AUS	80.84	97.2	0.00	599.54
	Mervyn Bennett (Regal Reign)		120.84	85.2	0.00	
	William Roycroft (Version)		86.66	128.8	0.00	
4	Euro Federico Roman (Shamrock)	ITA	73.34	120.8	0.00	682.24
	Mario Turner (Tempest Blisland)		99.59	113.6	0.00	
	Alessandro Argenton (Woodland)		102.91	172.0	0.00	
5	Yurii Salnikov (Rumpel)	URS	86.66	102.8	0.00	721.55
	Valerii Dvorianinov (Zeila)		86.25	122.0	10.00	
	Viktor Kalinin (Araks)		85.84	218.0	10.00	
6	Juliet Graham (Sumatra)	CAN	110.84	81.6	10.25	808.81
	Cathy Wedge (City Fella)		99.16	187.6	0.00	
	Robin Hahn (L'Esprit)		94.16	215.2	10.00	

Concours complet individuel		Three day event individual		Military Einzelwertung		Concorso completo individuale		
				Dressage Dressage Dressur Dressage		Epreuve de fond Endurance test Geländeritt Gara di fondo	Sauts d'obstacles Jumping Springen Salto ad ostacoli	
1	Edmund Coffin (Bally-Cor)	USA		64.59		50.4	0.00	114.99
2	John Plumb (Better&Better)	USA		66.25		49.6	10.00	125.85
3	Karl Schulz (Madrigal)	GER		46.25		63.2	20.00	129.45
4	Richard Meade (Jacob Jones)	GBR		73.75		57.6	10.00	141.35
5	Wayne Roycroft (Laurenson)	AUS		80.84		97.2	0.00	178.04
6	Gerard Sinnott (Croghan)	IRL		101.25		77.6	0.00	178.85
11	Juliet Graham (Sumatra)	CAN		110.84		81.6	10.25	202.69

Grand prix de dressage individuel Grosse Dressur Einzelwertung		Grand prix dressage individual Grand prix dressage individuale			Grand prix de sauts d'obstacles individuel Grosses Jagdspringen Einzelwertung		Grand prix jumping individual Salto ad ostacoli individuale	
1	Christine Stückelberger (Granat)	SUI	1486.0		1	Alwin Schockemohle (Warwick Rex)	GER	0.00
2	Harry Boldt (Woycek)	GER	1435.0		2	Michel Vaillancourt (Branch County)	CAN	(4.00) 12.00
3	Reiner Klimke (Mehmed)	GER	1395.0		3	François Mathy (Gai Luron)	BEL	(8.00) 12.00
4	Gabriela Grillo (Ultimo)	GER	1257.0		4	Debbie Johnsey (Moxy)	GBR	(15.25) 12.00
5	Dorothy Morkis (Monaco)	USA	1249.0		5	Guy Creighton, AUS, Hugo Simon (Mr. Dennis, Lavendee)	AUT	16.00
6	Viktor Ugriumov (Said)	URS	1247.0			Frank Chapot, USA, Marcel Rozier (Viscount, Bayard de Maupas)	FRA	
7	Chris Boylen (Gaspano)	CAN	1217.0		15	James Elder (Raffles II)	CAN	28.00
11	Lorraine Stubbs (True North)	CAN	1153.0		15	James Day (Sympatico)	CAN	28.00

Grand prix de dressage par équipe Grand prix dressage team Grosse Dressur Mannschaftswertung Grand prix dressage squadra					Grand prix de sauts d'obstacles par équipe Grand prix jumping team Preis der Nationen Manschaftswertung Salto ad ostacoli grand premio squadra			*indique pas compté indicates not counted	
1	Harry Boldt (Woycek) Reiner Klimke (Mehmed) Gabriela Grillo (Ultimo)	GER	1863.0 1751.0 1541.0	5155.0	1	Hubert Parot (Rivage) Marcel Rozier (Bayard de Maupas) Michel Roche (Un Espoir) Marc Roguet (Belle de Mars)	FRA	8.00 / 4.00 8.00 / 4.00 24.00*/ 8.00 8.00 /16.00*	40.00
2	Christine Stückelberger (Granat) Ulrich Lehmann (Widin) Doris Ramseier (Roch)	SUI	1869.0 1425.0 1390.0	4684.0	2	Hans G. Winkler (Torphy) Paul Schockemöhle (Agent) Alwin Schockemöhle (Warwick Rex) Sönke Sönksen (Kwepe)	GER	12.00 / 4.00 16.00 / 8.00 4.00 / 8.00 8.00 /12.00*	44.00
3	Hilda Gurney (Keen) Dorothy Morkis (Monaco) Edith Master (Dahlwitz)	USA	1607.0 1559.0 1481.0	4647.0	3	Eric Wauters (Gute Sitte) François Mathy (Gai Luron) Edgar Gupper (Le Champion) Stanny van Paeschen (Porsche)	BEL	8.00 / 7.00 12.00 / 8.00 12.00 /16.00 16.00*/20.00*	63.00
4	Viktor Ugriumov (Said) Ivan Kalita (Tarif) Ivan Kizimov (Rebus)	URS	1597.0 1520.0 1425.0	4542.0	4	Robert Ridland (South Side) Frank Chapot (Viscount) William Brown (Sandsablaze) Michael Matz (Grande)	USA	16.00*/ 4.00 12.00 / 4.00 12.00 /16.00 16.00 /24.00*	64.00
5	Chris Boylen (Gaspano) Lorraine Stubbs (True North) Barbara Stracey (Jungherr II)	CAN	1590.0 1549.0 1399.0	4538.0	5	Ian Millar (Countdown) Michel Vaillancourt (Branch County) James Day (Sympatico) James Elder (Raffles II)	CAN	19.50*/ 8.00 8.00 /12.50 4.00 /16.00 16.00 /20.00*	64.50
6	Ulla Petersen (Chigwell) Tony Jensen (Fox) Niels Haagensen (Lowenstern)	DEN	1552.0 1521.0 1375.0	4448.0	6	Luis Alvarez-Cervera (Acorne) Alfonso Segovia (Val de Loire) Jose Rosillo (Agamenon) Eduardo Amoros (Limited Edition)	ESP	8.00 / 8.00 11.00 /12.00 16.00*/20.00 12.00 /27.00*	71.00

Tir à l'arc/Archery/Bogenschiessen/Tiro all'arco

Dames	Ladies	Damen	Donne						
				70 m	60 m	50 m	30 m		
1	Luann Ryon		USA	578	625	618	678	RO/OR	2499
2	Valentina Kovpan		URS	589	626	559	686		2460
3	Zebiniso Rustamova		URS	564	603	580	660		2407
4	Sun Yong Jang		PRK	582	603	558	662		2405
5	Lucille Lemay		CAN	558	613	564	666		2401
6	Jadwiga Wilejto		POL	581	599	555	660		2395

			90 m	70 m	50 m	30 m		
1	Darrel Pace	USA	592	634	644	701	**RO/OR**	2571
2	Hiroshi Michinaga	JPN	575	615	613	699		2502
3	G. Carlo Ferrari	ITA	566	625	612	692		2495
4	Richard McKinney	USA	568	591	614	698		2471
5	Vladimir Chendarov	URS	540	617	616	694		2467
6	Willi Gabriel	GER	526	601	621	687		2435
7	Dave Mann	CAN	520	589	624	698		2431

Tir/Shooting/Schiessen/Tiro

1976   07-18/07-24

50 m	Pistolet libre Free pistol Scheibenpistole Pistola libera				
1	Uwe Potteck	GDR	**RM/WR**	573
2	Harald Vollmar	GDR		567
3	Rudolf Dollinger	AUT		562
4	Heinz Mertel	GER		560
5	Ragnar Skanaker	SWE		559
6	Vincenzo Tondo	ITA		559
23	Thomas Guinn	CAN		548

25 m	Pistolet de tir rapide Rapid fire pistol Schnellfeuer-Pistole Pistola automatica			
1	Norbert Klaar	GDR	297/300 **RO/OR**	597
2	Jürgen Wiefel	GDR	299/297	596
3	Roberto Ferraris	ITA	299/296	595
4	Afanasy Kuzmin	URS	298/297	595
5	Corneliu Ion	ROM	298/297	595
6	Erwin Glock	GER	296/298	594
31	Jules Sobrian	CAN	292/291	583

Carabine de petit calibre, position couchée Smallbore rifle, prone position			
1	Karlheinz Smieszek	GER	599
2	Ulrich Lind	GER	597
3	Gennady Lushchikov	URS	595

Kleinkaliber liegende stellung Carabina de piccolo calibro terra			
4	Anton Müller	SUI	595
5	Walter Frescura	ITA	594
6	Arne Sorensen	CAN	593
28	Hans Adlhoch	CAN	589

Carabine de petit calibre 3 positions   Smallbore Rifle 3 positions   Kleinkaliber dreistellungskampf   Carabina de piccolo calibro 3 posizione

			Couché / Prone / Liegend / Terra	Debout / Standing / Stehend / Piedi	Genoux / Kneeling / Knieend / Ginocchio	
1	Lanny Bassham	USA	397	373	392	1162
2	Margaret Murdock	USA	398	376	388	1162
3	Werner Seibold	GER	397	377	386	1160
4	Srecko Pejovic	YUG	391	379	386	1156
5	Sven Johansson	SWE	394	367	391	1152
6	Ho Jun Li	PRK	390	373	389	1152
14	Hans Adlhoch	CAN	393	365	386	1144

Fosse olympique Olympic trap shooting Trapschiessen Trap			
1	Donald Haldeman	USA	190
2	Armando Silva Marques	POR	189
3	Ubaldesc Baldi	ITA	189
4	Burckhardt Hoppe	GDR	186
5	Alexandr Androshkin	URS	185
6	Adam Smelczynski	POL	183
7	John Primrose	CAN	183

Skeet Skeet shooting Skeet-Schiessen Skeet			
1	Josef Panacek	TCH	198
2	Eric Swinkels	HOL	198
3	Wieslaw Gawlikowski	POL	196
4	Klaus Reschke	GDR	196
5	Franz Schitzhofer	AUT	195
6	Edgardo Zachrisson	GUA	194
35	Harry Willsie	CAN	188

Cible courante Running game target Laufende Scheibe Bersaglio mobile				
1	Alexandr Gazov	URS	287/292 **RM/WR**	579
2	Alexandr Kedyarov	URS	292/284	576
3	Jerry Greszkiewicz	POL	285/286	571
4	Thomas Pfeffer	GDR	289/282	571
5	Wolfgang Hamberger	GER	292/275	567
6	Helmut Bellingrodt	COL	282/285	567
25	Daniel Nadeau	CAN	267/259	526

Yachting/Yachting/Segeln/Vela

Finn

1	J. Schümann	GDR	35.40
2	A. Balashov	URS	39.70
3	J. Bertrand	AUS	46.40
4	C. Biekarck	BRA	54.70
5	K. Carlson	SWE	66.40
6	A. Boudouris	GRE	77.00
8	S. Riley	CAN	83.00

Flying Dutchman

1	J. Diesch/E. Diesch	GER	34.70
2	R. Pattisson/J. Brooke-Houghton	GBR	51.70
3	R. Conrad/P. Ficker	BRA	52.10
4	H. Fogh/E. Bastet	CAN	57.10
5	V. Leontiev/V. Zubanov	URS	59.40
6	N. Freeman/J. Mathias	USA	65.70

International 470

1	F. Hübner/H. Bode	GER	42.40
2	A. Gorostegui/P. Millet	ESP	49.70
3	I. Brown/I. Ruff	AUS	57.00
4	V. Potapov/A. Potapov	URS	57.00
5	M. Paterson/B. Bennett	NZL	59.70
6	P. Grebbin/D. Clark	GBR	69.40
16	C. Park/J. Cross	CAN	109.70

Soling

1	P. Jensen/V. Bandolowski/E. Hansen	DEN	46.70
2	J. Kolius/W. Glasgow/R. Hoepfner	USA	47.40
3	D. Below/M. Zachries/O. Engelhardt	GDR	47.40
4	B. Budnikov/V. Zamotaikin/N. Poliakov	URS	48.70
5	G. Bakker/H. de Vlaming/P. Keijzer	HOL	58.00
6	W. Kuhweide/K. Meyer/A. May	GER	60.70
8	G. Dexter/S. McMillan/A. Josenhans	CAN	68.70

Tempest

1	J. Albrechtson/I. Hansson	SWE	14.00
2	V. Mankin/V. Akimenko	URS	30.40
3	D. Conner/C. Findlay	USA	32.70
4	U. Mares/W. Stadler	GER	42.10
5	G. Milone/R. Mottola	ITA	55.40
6	Cl. Christensen/F. Christensen	DEN	62.70
7	A. Leibel/L. Leibel	CAN	65.10

Tornado

1	R. White/J. Osborn	GBR	18.00
2	D. McFaull/M. Rothwell	USA	36.00
3	J. Spengler/J. Schmall	GER	37.70
4	B. Lewis/W. Rock	AUS	44.40
5	P. Kolni/J. Kolni	SWE	57.40
6	W. Steiner/A. Schiess	SUI	63.40
7	L. Woods/M. de la Roche	CAN	69.70

Basketball/Basketball/Basketball/Pallacanestro

Dames   Ladies   Damen   Donne

		URS	USA	BUL	TCH	JPN	CAN	CAN:
1	URS		112: 77	91: 68	88: 75	98: 75	115: 51	J. Douthwright, J. Sargent, A. Hurley,
2	USA	77:112		95: 79	83: 67	71: 84	89: 75	Ch. Critelli, B. Bland, C. Dufresne,
3	BUL	68: 91	79: 95		67: 66	66: 63	85: 62	S. Strike, S. Sweeney, C. Turney,
4	TCH	75: 88	67: 83	66: 67		76: 62	67: 59	D. Hobin, A. Johnson, B. Barnes
5	JPN	75: 98	84: 71	63: 66	62: 76		121: 89	
6	CAN	51:115	75: 89	62: 85	59: 67	89:121		

Messieurs   Men   Herren   Uomini

		USA	YUG	URS	CAN	ITA	TCH	CAN:
1	USA		95: 74					A. Devlin, M. Riley, B. Robinson,
2	YUG	74: 95						J. Cassidy, D. Sankey, R. Sharpe,
3	URS				100: 72			C. Hall, J. Russell, R. Town, R. Raffin,
4	CAN			72:100				L. Hansen, P. Tollestrup
5	ITA						98: 75	
6	TCH				75: 98			

Football/Football/Fussball/Calcio

		GDR	POL	URS	BRA	CAN	CAN:
1	GDR		3:1			huitièmes de finale	J. Brand, B. Bolitho, R. Telford,
2	POL	1:3				eighth-finals	K. Grant, T. Lawrence, J. Douglas,
3	URS				2:0		J. McGrane, R. Megraw, C. Rose,
4	BRA			0:2			J. Connor, M. McLeneghan,
							W. McLeod, G. Ayrel, P. Roe,
							T. Lettieri, J. McLoughlin,
							K. Whitehead

Handball/Handball/Handball/Pallamano

Dames   Ladies   Damen   Donne

		URS	GDR	HUN	ROM	JPN	CAN	CAN:
1	URS		14: 11	12: 9	14: 8	31: 9	21: 3	D. Chenard, L. Hurtubise,
2	GDR	11: 14		7: 7	18: 12	24: 10	29: 4	D. Lemaire, F. Boulay-Parizeau,
3	HUN	9: 12	7: 7		20: 15	25: 18	24: 3	J. Rail, N. Genier, L. Balthazar,
4	ROM	8: 14	12: 18	15: 20		21: 20	17: 11	M. Charette, M. Prud'Homme,
5	JPN	9: 31	10: 24	18: 25	20: 21		15: 14	L. Beaumont, M. Houle, N. Robert,
6	CAN	3: 21	4: 29	3: 24	11: 17	14: 15		J. Valois, H. Tetreault

Messieurs   Men   Herren   Uomini

		URS	ROM	POL	GER	YUG	HUN	CAN:
1	URS		19: 15					C. Lefebvre, Ch. Chagnon, P. Ferdais,
2	ROM	15: 19						R. Johnson, P. Desormeaux, C. Viens, R.
3	POL				21: 18			Lambert, P. St. Martin, H. De Roussan,
4	GER			18: 21				F. Dauphin, D. Power, L. Tousignant,
5	YUG						21: 19	W. Blankenau, S. Thorseth
6	HUN					19: 21		
11	CAN							

Hockey/Hockey/Hockey/Hockey

		NZL	AUS	PAK	HOL	GER	ESP	CAN:
1	NZL		1:0					J. Macdougall, S. Dusang, D. Bissett,
2	AUS	0:1						A. Hobkirk, R. Plummer, L. Wright,
3	PAK				3:2			L. Carey, P. Motzek, D. Pready,
4	HOL			2:3				K. Wood, P. Lown, F. Hoos, B. Chohan,
5	GER						9:1	M. Mouat, K. Gosal, A. Schouten
6	ESP					1:9		
10	CAN							

Volleyball/Volleyball/Volleyball/Volleyball

Dames   Ladies   Damen   Donne

		JPN	URS	KOR	HUN	CUB	GDR
1	JPN		3:0				
2	URS	0:3					
3	KOR				3:1		
4	HUN			1:3			
5	CUB						3:0
6	GDR					0:3	
8	CAN						

CAN: C. Bishop, B. Dalton, K. Girvan, P. Olson,
R. Armanas, A. Ireland, M. Dempster, C. Lloyd,
B. Baxter, C. Lebrun, D. Heeps, A. Vandervelden

Messieurs   Men   Herren   Uomini

		POL	URS	CUB	JPN	TCH	KOR
1	POL		3:2				
2	URS	2:3					
3	CUB				3:0		
4	JPN			0:3			
5	TCH						3:1
6	KOR					1:3	
9	CAN						

CAN: G. Russell, A. Taylor, E. Romanchych,
D. Michalski, G. Pischke, K. Klostermann, B. Prasil,
L. Plenart, P. Belanger, E. Alexiuk, T. Graham, J. Paulsen

Water Polo/Water Polo/Wasserball/Pallanuoto

		HUN	ITA	HOL	ROM	YUG	GER	CAN:
1	HUN		6:5	5:3	9:8	5:5	5:3	G. Leclerc, G. Csepregi, D. Hart,
2	ITA	5:6		3:3	4:4	5:4	4:3	P. Pottier, G. Turcotte, C. Barry,
3	HOL	3:5	3:3		4:4	5:3	3:2	J. Ducharme, P. Pugliese,
4	ROM	8:9	4:4	4:4		5:5	5:3	G. Gross, J. Mcleod, D. Dion
5	YUG	5:5	4:5	3:5	5:5		4:4	
6	GER	3:5	3:4	2:3	3:5	4:4		
9	CAN							